Learn by *Heart* Poetry

Learn by Heart Poetry

Verse to enjoy and cherish for life

ARCTURUS

About George Davidson

George Davidson studied modern languages and linguistics at the universities of Glasgow, Edinburgh and Strasbourg, and is a graduate of Edinburgh University. A former senior editor with Chambers Harrap Publishers Ltd, he is now a freelance compiler and editor of dictionaries and other reference books. He lives in Edinburgh.

Credits

We would like to thank the following people for permission to reproduce poems in this book: The Society of Authors: *The Listeners* by Walter de la Mare (page 67), *Cargoes* and *Sea Fever* by John Masefield (pages 145 and 146) and *I Meant to Do My Work Today* by Richard Le Gallienne (page 122). Alison C. Webster: *On a Cat, Ageing* by Sir Alexander Gray (page 80). *Dreams* by Langston Hughes (page 92) from *The Collected Poems of Langston Hughes*, Alfred A Knopf Inc. *Song at the Beginning of Autumn* by Elizabeth Jennings (page 94) from *Collected Poems* by Carcanet. Johnson and Alcock Ltd: *Warning* by Jenny Joseph (page 97). The Royal Literary Fund: *The Naming of Parts* by Henry Reed (page 169). Anne Longepe: *Each Day a Life* by Robert Service (page 182).

ARCTURUS

This edition published in 2014 by Arcturus Publishing Limited
26/27 Bickels Yard, 151–153 Bermondsey Street,
London SE1 3HA

Copyright © 2013 Arcturus Publishing Limited

ISBN: 978-1-78212-869-4
AD003945UK

Printed in China

Contents

John Masefield

John McCrae

Charlotte Mew

Moina Michael

Clement Clarke Moore

E Nesbit

Edgar Allan Poe

Alexander Pope

Henry Reed

Christina Rossetti

Dante Gabriel Rossetti

Frederick George Scott

Introduction

For many of us, the only experience we have had of learning poetry was during our schooldays, and, again for many of us, it was not a particularly pleasurable or rewarding experience. We were given poems or, perhaps, passages of Shakespeare to learn, regardless of whether or not we liked or even understood them, and usually with no explanation as to why we should learn them or what benefit it would bring us. Learning such pieces was a dull and difficult chore. And yet . . . so often, when we did find a poem we liked, a poem that caught our attention or fired our imagination, how easy it was to learn. That was certainly my experience with Robert Browning's poem *My Last Duchess*: I didn't set out to learn it at school, and I wasn't forced to, but I liked the poem so much and read it so many times for pleasure that I found that I had indeed memorized it, without effort.

This, I believe, is the key to both why and how we can all learn poetry by heart. But the question may still be asked, why should we? Many worthy reasons have been put forward for memorizing poetry: for example, preserving and passing on our cultural heritage, enhancing our written and spoken language skills, improving our memory. But in my opinion these are of secondary importance and indeed almost beside the point: first and foremost, we should learn poetry simply because we want to learn it. We should learn a poem because we like it, because we have enjoyed reading it, because it speaks to us, because it makes us laugh or cry, because it brings us solace or reassurance, because it gives us a better understanding of ourselves or of other people, because it brings back memories of childhood, or for any of a dozen other personal reasons. We should learn a poem because – for whatever reason – we want to have it with us as a readily available companion in all that life brings us or throws at us.

This I have kept constantly in mind as I have been making my choice of poems for this anthology. It is, inevitably, a personal choice, but nonetheless in making my selection my thought has always been: 'Is this a poem other people will enjoy reading? Is this a poem other people might want to learn?' This is a book of poetry in which I hope every reader will find not only 'old friends' that they remember, or perhaps only half-remember, from childhood and school, but also some 'new acquaintances' – poets and poems they have never come across before.

As you will see from the contents pages or by flicking through the pages of the book itself, there is wide range of poetry here, both ancient (though not too ancient – all the poems are in modern English, with the exception of three by Robert Burns which are of course in Scots) and modern. In making my selection I have chosen poetry from three broad categories:

- well-known poems by well-known poets;
- less well-known poems by well-known poets; and
- good poems by less well-known poets.

This, I feel, has made for an interesting mixture of poetry, with something that will appeal to everyone. There are short poems, medium-length poems and some quite long poems (I have not assumed that readers will only want to learn short poems – some may relish the challenge of a longer piece; and even for those who do not, there is pleasure and satisfaction in learning even just part of a long poem). There are poems about life and love, poems about war and death, poems about seasons and ships and solitude, serious poems and humorous poems. (You will find an index by topic on pages 246–256.) There are poems you would expect to find in an anthology such as this, but I hope there will also be some surprises. And while it is unlikely that any reader will attempt to *learn* all the poems in this anthology, I hope that everyone will at least enjoy *reading* all the poems collected here.

Along with the poems, I have included brief notes on the poets and, where I felt it to be useful or interesting, about the poems themselves. There is little point in learning a poem if you don't really understand what it is about. For those who want more information about the poets and poems than could be covered in the notes, there are many useful websites that can be searched online. You can even hear some of the poems being recited.

We have spoken about *why* you should learn poetry: let's now turn our attention to *how* to learn poetry. Let's say you have found a poem you want to learn. How should you set about it? If you are not used to learning poetry (or anything else) by heart, then you would be wise not to bite off too much at your first attempt. If there are a number of poems you hope to learn, start with one that is not too long: you want the buzz and satisfaction of quick success to buoy you up and encourage you to continue. Perhaps choose a poem you half-remember – it will be easier to learn because you already know some of it. Read the poem over several times. (In fact, you have probably already done that, because you like the poem.) Then start to learn it line by line from the beginning. Once you start, try to learn at least a line or two every day, and if possible set aside a regular time when you can work at it. (Well, perhaps 'work' is not the right word here – don't think of it as *work* – learning poetry has to be fun.) There is, of course, no universally correct time of the day for this – larks and owls will each have to find the time of day that suits them best. One learning method is to write out the lines several times, as many times as you need, to memorize the words. Or you may find it easier to say the lines out loud to yourself while pacing up and down the room in the rhythm of the poem. Let the rhythm and the rhymes of the poem help you. (There is no one correct method here – whatever works for you *is* the correct method, and you will have to establish that for yourself.) You could record or download the poem and play it back to yourself while travelling to and from work, or when out jogging, or while doing housework. Visualizing what the poem describes, verse by verse or scene by scene, is helpful, especially with a long poem. Relate key words to key pictures in your mind.

Don't forget to check that you have not forgotten what you have already learned, before adding on the next couple of lines. There may be days when you only have time to remind yourself of what you already know, or need to go back and relearn words or lines you don't quite remember. This is useful, too, so don't be disappointed when it happens. Don't give up – you *will* get there in the end. And you will find that the more you learn, the easier it becomes.

Lastly, you may start with this book, but don't limit yourself to it. If you find a poet here whose work you like, head for the bookshop or library to discover more! There's a lot of great poetry out there.

George Davidson

The Fairies

William Allingham (1824–1889)

William Allingham was born in County Donegal, in the northwest of Ireland. A customs officer by profession, he wrote several volumes of poetry.

Up the airy mountain,
  Down the rushy glen,
We daren't go a-hunting
  For fear of little men;
Wee folk, good folk,
  Trooping all together;
Green jacket, red cap
  And white owl's feather.

Down along the rocky shore
  Some make their home,
They live on crispy pancakes
  Of yellow tide-foam;
Some in the reeds
  Of the black mountain-lake,
With frogs for their watch-dogs,
  All night awake.

High on the hill-top
  The old King sits;
He is now so old and gray
  He's nigh lost his wits.
With a bridge of white mist
  Columbkill he crosses,
On his stately journeys
  From Slieveleague to Rosses;
Or going up with music,
  On cold starry nights,
To sup with the Queen
  Of the gay Northern Lights.

They stole little Bridget
  For seven years long;
When she came down again
  Her friends were all gone.
They took her lightly back
  Between the night and morrow;
They thought she was fast asleep,
  But she was dead with sorrow.
They have kept her ever since
  Deep within the lake,
On a bed of flag-leaves,
  Watching till she wake.

By the craggy hill-side,
  Through the mosses bare,
They have planted thorn-trees
  For pleasure here and there.
Is any man so daring
  As dig them up in spite,
He shall find their sharpest thorns
  In his bed at night.

Up the airy mountain
  Down the rushy glen,
We daren't go a-hunting,
  For fear of little men;
Wee folk, good folk,
  Trooping all together;
Green jacket, red cap,
  And white owl's feather.

Columbkill, Slieveleague and the Rosses are
respectively a valley, a coastal mountain and a
district in Donegal.
  Notice that each verse of this poem paints a
separate picture. Take the poem a verse at a time,
and as a memory aid visualize each picture before
you start to memorize the verse. Note also the
rhyme scheme of each stanza – being aware of
which lines rhyme with each other is another useful
aid to memorizing a poem. (You can apply these
tips to several of the poems in this anthology.)

Dover Beach

Matthew Arnold (1822–1888)

Matthew Arnold was an English poet and critic. This
poem combines a description of the view over the
English Channel towards France with thoughts on
life, faith and love, and with the melancholy which
features in much of Arnold's poetry.
  The Sea of Faith religious network takes its name
from the reference to the 'Sea of Faith' in the third
stanza of the poem.

The sea is calm to-night.
The tide is full, the moon lies fair
Upon the straits; — on the French coast the light
Gleams and is gone; the cliffs of England stand,
Glimmering and vast, out in the tranquil bay.
Come to the window, sweet is the night-air!
Only, from the long line of spray
Where the sea meets the moon-blanched land,
Listen! you hear the grating roar
Of pebbles which the waves draw back, and fling,
At their return, up the high strand,
Begin, and cease, and then again begin,
With tremulous cadence slow, and bring
The eternal note of sadness in.

Sophocles long ago
Heard it on the Ægean, and it brought
Into his mind the turbid ebb and flow
Of human misery; we
Find also in the sound a thought,
Hearing it by this distant northern sea.

The Sea of Faith
Was once, too, at the full, and round earth's shore
Lay like the folds of a bright girdle furled.
But now I only hear
Its melancholy, long, withdrawing roar,
Retreating, to the breath
Of the night-wind, down the vast edges drear
And naked shingles of the world.

Ah, love, let us be true
To one another! for the world, which seems
To lie before us like a land of dreams,
So various, so beautiful, so new,
Hath really neither joy, nor love, nor light,
Nor certitude, nor peace, nor help for pain;
And we are here as on a darkling plain
Swept with confused alarms of struggle and flight,
Where ignorant armies clash by night.

Little Hands

Laurence Binyon (1869–1943)

Laurence Binyon is best known for his war poem *For the Fallen*, which includes the famous lines:
   "They shall grow not old, as we that are left grow old:
Age shall not weary them, nor the years condemn.
At the going down of the sun and in the morning
We will remember them."
   However, the poem chosen for inclusion in this anthology paints a much happier picture.

Soft little hands that stray and clutch,
Like fern fronds curl and uncurl bold,
While baby faces lie in such
Close sleep as flowers at night that fold,
What is it you would clasp and hold,
Wandering outstretched with wilful touch?
O fingers small of shell-tipped rose,
How should you know you hold so much?
Two full hearts beating you inclose,
Hopes, fears, prayers, longings, joys and woes, —
All yours to hold, O little hands!
More, more than wisdom understands
And love, love only knows.

The Lamb

William Blake (1757–1827)

> William Blake was an English poet who was also a painter and engraver and a Christian mystic. *The Lamb* and the following poem, *The Tyger*, complement each other, describing two aspects of God's creation as Blake saw it – its gentleness and its ferocity. As Blake in wonder asks the tiger, 'Did he who made the lamb make thee?'

Little Lamb who made thee?
   Dost thou know who made thee?
Gave thee life and bid thee feed
By the stream and o'er the mead;
Gave thee clothing of delight,
Softest clothing woolly bright;
Gave thee such a tender voice,
Making all the vales rejoice.
   Little Lamb who made thee?
   Dost thou know who made thee?

Little Lamb I'll tell thee,
Little Lamb I'll tell thee:
He is called by thy name,
For he calls himself a lamb:
He is meek and he is mild,
He became a little child.
I a child and thou a lamb,
We are called by his name.
Little Lamb God bless thee.
Little Lamb God bless thee.

Note that in the third line of the second stanza,
'called' has to be pronounced with two syllables in
order to preserve the rhythm of the poem.

The Tyger

William Blake

Tyger, tyger, burning bright
In the forests of the night:
What immortal hand or eye
Could frame thy fearful symmetry?

In what distant deeps or skies
Burnt the fire of thine eyes?
On what wings dare he aspire?
What the hand dare seize the fire?

And what shoulder, and what art,
Could twist the sinews of thy heart?
And when thy heart began to beat,
What dread hand? and what dread feet?

What the hammer? what the chain?
In what furnace was thy brain?
What the anvil? what dread grasp
Dare its deadly terrors clasp?

When the stars threw down their spears,
And watered Heaven with their tears,
Did he smile his work to see?
Did he who made the lamb make thee?

Tyger, tyger, burning bright
In the forests of the night:
What immortal hand or eye
Dare frame thy fearful symmetry?

To My Dear and Loving Husband

Anne Bradstreet (c.1612–1672)

Anne Bradstreet was born in England but sailed to America with her husband and other Puritans when she was in her late teens. She was one of the first poets in the American colonies.

If ever two were one, then surely we.
If ever man were lov'd by wife, then thee;
If ever wife was happy in a man,
Compare with me ye women if you can.
I prize thy love more than whole mines of gold,
Or all the riches that the East doth hold.
My love is such that rivers cannot quench,
Nor ought but love from thee give recompence.
Thy love is such I can no way repay,
The heavens reward thee manifold I pray.
Then while we live, in love let's so persever,
That when we live no more, we may live ever.

Notice the old spelling and pronunciation of *persever* (also found in Shakespeare), stressed on the second syllable and rhyming with *ever*.

London Snow

Robert Bridges (1844–1930)

Robert Bridges was an English poet and critic. He
was appointed Poet Laureate in 1913.

When men were all asleep the snow came flying,
In large white flakes falling on the city brown,
Stealthily and perpetually settling and loosely lying,
   Hushing the latest traffic of the drowsy town;
Deadening, muffling, stifling its murmurs failing;
Lazily and incessantly floating down and down:
   Silently sifting and veiling road, roof and railing;
Hiding difference, making unevenness even,
Into angles and crevices softly drifting and sailing.
   All night it fell, and when full inches seven
It lay in the depth of its uncompacted lightness,
The clouds blew off from a high and frosty heaven;
   And all woke earlier for the unaccustomed brightness
Of the winter dawning, the strange unheavenly glare:
The eye marvelled — marvelled at the dazzling
   whiteness;
   The ear hearkened to the stillness of the solemn air;
No sound of wheel rumbling nor of foot falling,
And the busy morning cries came thin and spare.
   Then boys I heard, as they went to school, calling,

They gathered up the crystal manna to freeze
Their tongues with tasting, their hands with snowballing;
   Or rioted in a drift, plunging up to the knees;
Or peering up from under the white-mossed wonder,
'O look at the trees!' they cried, 'O look at the trees!'
   With lessened load a few carts creak and blunder,
Following along the white deserted way,
A country company long dispersed asunder:
   When now already the sun, in pale display
Standing by Paul's high dome, spread forth below
His sparkling beams, and awoke the stir of the day.
   For now doors open, and war is waged with the snow;
And trains of sombre men, past tale of number,
Tread long brown paths, as toward their toil they go:
   But even for them awhile no cares encumber
Their minds diverted; the daily word is unspoken,
The daily thoughts of labour and sorrow slumber
At the sight of the beauty that greets them, for the
    charm they have broken.

'Paul's high dome' = the dome of St Paul's
Cathedral in London.
   Picture the snow as it falls during the night,
and the scene as the city wakes to discover it
in the morning. As the poem is not divided into
convenient stanzas for learning, look for small
sections you can learn easily one at a time: for
example, the first four lines, to 'drowsy town'; then
the next five, to 'drifting and sailing', and so on.

Nightingales

Robert Bridges

Beautiful must be the mountains whence ye come,
And bright in the fruitful valleys the streams, wherefrom
    Ye learn your song:
Where are those starry woods? O might I wander there,
  Among the flowers, which in that heavenly air
    Bloom the year long!

Nay, barren are those mountains and spent the streams:
  Our song is the voice of desire, that haunts our dreams,
    A throe of the heart,
Whose pining visions dim, forbidden hopes profound,
  No dying cadence nor long sigh can sound,
    For all our art.

Alone, aloud in the raptured ear of men
  We pour our dark nocturnal secret; and then,
    As night is withdrawn
From these sweet-springing meads and bursting boughs
  of May,
  Dream, while the innumerable choir of day
    Welcome the dawn.

 Stanza 1 is said by the poet to the nightingales; stanzas 2 and 3 by the nightingales to the poet.

The Soldier

Rupert Brooke (1887–1915)

Rupert Brooke died of septicaemia on a ship en route to Gallipoli. The 'corner of a foreign field' where he is buried is on the Greek island of Skyros.

If I should die, think only this of me:
  That there's some corner of a foreign field
That is for ever England. There shall be
  In that rich earth a richer dust concealed;
A dust whom England bore, shaped, made aware,
  Gave, once, her flowers to love, her ways to roam,
A body of England's, breathing English air,
  Washed by the rivers, blest by suns of home.

And think, this heart, all evil shed away,
  A pulse in the eternal mind, no less
    Gives somewhere back the thoughts by England given;
Her sights and sounds; dreams happy as her day;
  And laughter, learnt of friends; and gentleness,
    In hearts at peace, under an English heaven.

This 14-line poem is a sonnet. It is a good poem for beginners to learn – not too long, and with a rhyme scheme that acts as a useful memory aid.

How Do I Love Thee?

Elizabeth Barrett Browning (1806–1861)

Elizabeth Barrett Browning was the wife of the poet Robert Browning. They married in secret and left England to live in Italy. This poem and the next one are taken from Elizabeth Browning's love poems *Sonnets from the Portuguese*. Despite the title, they are original works, not translations.

How do I love thee? Let me count the ways.
I love thee to the depth and breadth and height
My soul can reach, when feeling out of sight
For the ends of Being and ideal Grace.
I love thee to the level of every day's
Most quiet need, by sun and candlelight.
I love thee freely, as men strive for Right;
I love thee purely, as they turn from Praise.
I love thee with a passion put to use
In my old griefs, and with my childhood's faith.
I love thee with a love I seemed to lose
With my lost saints, — I love thee with the breath,
Smiles, tears, of all my life! — and, if God choose,
I shall but love thee better after death.

Like Brooke's *The Soldier* (see page 31), this is a sonnet. If you are using rhyme schemes as a memory aid, notice that the rhyme scheme here is not the same as the one Brooke uses. Sonnets always have 14 lines, but different poets use different rhyme patterns.

If Thou Must Love Me

Elizabeth Barrett Browning

If thou must love me, let it be for naught
Except for love's sake only. Do not say
'I love her for her smile … her look … her way
Of speaking gently, … for a trick of thought
That falls in well with mine, and certes brought
A sense of pleasant ease on such a day' —
For these things in themselves, Belovèd, may
Be changed, or change for thee, — and love, so
   wrought,
May be unwrought so. Neither love me for
Thine own dear pity's wiping my cheeks dry, —
A creature might forget to weep, who bore
Thy comfort long, and lose thy love thereby!
But love me for love's sake, that evermore
Thou may'st love on, through love's eternity.

Song

Elizabeth Barrett Browning

Weep, as if you thought of laughter!
Smile, as tears were coming after!
Marry your pleasures to your woes;
And think life's green well worth its rose!

No sorrow will your heart betide,
Without a comfort by its side;
The sun may sleep in his sea-bed,
But you have starlight overhead.

Trust not to joy! the rose of June,
When opened wide, will wither soon;
Italian days without twilight
Will turn them suddenly to night.

Joy, most changeful of all things,
Flits away on rainbow wings;
And when they look the gayest, know,
It is that they are spread to go!

The Lady's Yes

Elizabeth Barrett Browning

'Yes,' I answered you last night;
  'No,' this morning, sir, I say.
Colours seen by candle-light,
  Will not look the same by day.

When the viols played their best,
  Lamps above and laughs below,
Love me sounded like a jest,
  Fit for *yes* or fit for *no*.

Call me false or call me free,
  Vow, whatever light may shine,
No man on your face shall see
  Any grief for change on mine.

Yet the sin is on us both;
  Time to dance is not to woo;
Wooer light makes fickle troth,
  Scorn of *me* recoils on *you*.

Learn to win a lady's faith
  Nobly, as the thing is high,
Bravely, as for life and death,
  With a loyal gravity.

Lead her from the festive boards,
 Point her to the starry skies;
Guard her, by your truthful words,
 Pure from courtship's flatteries.

By your truth she shall be true,
 Ever true, as wives of yore,
And her yes, once said to you,
 Shall be *Yes* for evermore.

How They Brought the Good News from Ghent to Aix

Robert Browning (1812–1889)

I sprang to the stirrup, and Joris, and he;
I galloped, Dirck galloped, we galloped all three;
'Good speed!' cried the watch, as the gate-bolts undrew;
'Speed!' echoed the wall to us galloping through;
Behind shut the postern, the lights sank to rest,
And into the midnight we galloped abreast.

Not a word to each other; we kept the great pace
Neck by neck, stride by stride, never changing our place;
I turned in my saddle and made its girths tight,
Then shortened each stirrup, and set the pique right,
Rebuckled the cheek-strap, chained slacker the bit,
Nor galloped less steadily Roland a whit.

'Twas moonset at starting; but while we drew near
Lokeren, the cocks crew and twilight dawned clear;
At Boom, a great yellow star came out to see;
At Düffeld, 'twas morning as plain as could be;
And from Mecheln church-steeple we heard the half-chime,
So Joris broke silence with, 'Yet there is time!'

At Aershot, up leaped of a sudden the sun,
And against him the cattle stood black every one,
To stare thro' the mist at us galloping past,
And I saw my stout galloper Roland at last,
With resolute shoulders, each butting away
The haze, as some bluff river headland its spray:

And his low head and crest, just one sharp ear bent back
For my voice, and the other pricked out on his track;
And one eye's black intelligence, — ever that glance
O'er its white edge at me, his own master, askance!
And the thick heavy spume-flakes which aye and anon
His fierce lips shook upwards in galloping on.

By Hasselt, Dirck groaned; and cried Joris, 'Stay spur!
'Your Roos galloped bravely, the fault's not in her,
'We'll remember at Aix' — for one heard the quick
　wheeze
Of her chest, saw the stretched neck and staggering knees,
And sunk tail, and horrible heave of the flank,
As down on her haunches she shuddered and sank.

So, we were left galloping, Joris and I,
Past Looz and past Tongres, no cloud in the sky;
The broad sun above laughed a pitiless laugh,
'Neath our feet broke the brittle bright stubble like chaff;
Till over by Dalhem a dome-spire sprang white,
And 'Gallop,' gasped Joris, 'for Aix is in sight!'

'How they'll greet us!' — and all in a moment his roan
Rolled neck and croup over, lay dead as a stone;
And there was my Roland to bear the whole weight
Of the news which alone could save Aix from her fate,
With his nostrils like pits full of blood to the brim,
And with circles of red for his eye-sockets' rim.

Then I cast loose my buffcoat, each holster let fall,
Shook off both my jack-boots, let go belt and all,
Stood up in the stirrup, leaned, patted his ear,
Called my Roland his pet-name, my horse without peer;
Clapped my hands, laughed and sang, any noise,
　bad or good,
Till at length into Aix Roland galloped and stood.

And all I remember is — friends flocking round
As I sat with his head 'twixt my knees on the ground;
And no voice but was praising this Roland of mine,
As I poured down his throat our last measure of wine,
Which (the burgesses voted by common consent)
Was no more than his due who brought good news from
    Ghent.

Robert Browning was one of the most popular
English poets of the 19th century. As Browning
readily admitted, there is no historical foundation
to this tale of an urgent ride from Ghent to Aix,
and what the 'good news' might be is left to the
reader's imagination. As with other poems of this
type and length, it is best to read it over several
times and visualize the story stanza by stanza. Then
tackle each stanza in turn until you have mastered
the whole tale.
   'Set the pique' in the second stanza means to
adjust the saddle.

My Last Duchess

Robert Browning

> The speaker here is Alfonso II (1533–1597), fifth
> Duke of Ferrara. In 1558, he married 14-year-old
> Lucrezia de' Medici. She died three years later,
> probably of TB, though there were rumours of
> poisoning. Browning said he had in mind that she
> had either been murdered or shut up in a convent.

That's my last Duchess painted on the wall,
Looking as if she were alive. I call
That piece a wonder, now: Frà Pandolf's hands
Worked busily a day, and there she stands.
Will't please you sit and look at her? I said
'Frà Pandolf' by design, for never read
Strangers like you that pictured countenance,
The depth and passion of its earnest glance,
But to myself they turned (since none puts by
The curtain I have drawn for you, but I)
And seemed as they would ask me, if they durst,
How such a glance came there; so, not the first
Are you to turn and ask thus. Sir, 'twas not
Her husband's presence only, called that spot
Of joy into the Duchess' cheek: perhaps
Frà Pandolf chanced to say 'Her mantle laps
Over my lady's wrist too much,' or 'Paint
Must never hope to reproduce the faint

Half-flush that dies along her throat': such stuff
Was courtesy, she thought, and cause enough
For calling up that spot of joy. She had
A heart — how shall I say? — too soon made glad,
Too easily impressed; she liked whate'er
She looked on, and her looks went everywhere.
Sir, 'twas all one! My favour at her breast,
The dropping of the daylight in the West,
The bough of cherries some officious fool
Broke in the orchard for her, the white mule
She rode with round the terrace — all and each
Would draw from her alike the approving speech,
Or blush, at least. She thanked men, — good! but thanked
Somehow — I know not how — as if she ranked
My gift of a nine-hundred-years-old name
With anybody's gift. Who'd stoop to blame
This sort of trifling? Even had you skill
In speech — (which I have not) — to make your will
Quite clear to such an one, and say, 'Just this
Or that in you disgusts me; here you miss,
Or there exceed the mark' — and if she let
Herself be lessoned so, nor plainly set
Her wits to yours, forsooth, and made excuse,
— E'en then would be some stooping; and I choose
Never to stoop. Oh sir, she smiled, no doubt,
Whene'er I passed her; but who passed without
Much the same smile? This grew; I gave commands;
Then all smiles stopped together. There she stands
As if alive. Will't please you rise? We'll meet
The company below, then. I repeat,

The Count your master's known munificence
Is ample warrant that no just pretence
Of mine for dowry will be disallowed;
Though his fair daughter's self, as I avowed
At starting, is my object. Nay, we'll go
Together down, sir. Notice Neptune, though,
Taming a sea-horse, thought a rarity,
Which Claus of Innsbruck cast in bronze for me!

Notice that although the poem rhymes, the rhymes generally do not come at the ends of sentences. The poem flows across line ends, a technique which drives it on as the Duke unwittingly reveals more and more of his character and the probable fate of his previous wife.

Home Thoughts, from Abroad

Robert Browning

Oh, to be in England
Now that April's there,
And whoever wakes in England
Sees, some morning, unaware,
That the lowest boughs and the brushwood sheaf
Round the elm-tree bole are in tiny leaf,
While the chaffinch sings on the orchard bough
In England — now!

And after April, when May follows,
And the whitethroat builds, and all the swallows!
Hark, where my blossomed pear-tree in the hedge
Leans to the field and scatters on the clover
Blossoms and dewdrops — at the bent spray's edge —
That's the wise thrush; he sings each song twice over,
Lest you should think he never could recapture
The first fine careless rapture!
And though the fields look rough with hoary dew,
All will be gay when noontide wakes anew
The buttercups, the little children's dower
— Far brighter than this gaudy melon-flower!

Ae Fond Kiss

Robert Burns (1759–1796)

This is the last poem Burns wrote to Agnes M'Lehose, with whom he was close, before she set sail for Jamaica. They never met again.

Ae fond kiss, and then we sever;
Ae fareweel, and then for ever!
Deep in heart-wrung tears I'll pledge thee,
Warring sighs and groans I'll wage thee.

Who shall say that Fortune grieves him,
While the star of hope she leaves him?
Me, nae cheerfu' twinkle lights me;
Dark despair around benights me.

I'll ne'er blame my partial fancy,
Naething could resist my Nancy:
But to see her, was to love her;
Love but her, and love for ever.

Had we never lov'd sae kindly,
Had we never lov'd sae blindly,
Never met — or never parted,
We had ne'er been broken-hearted.

Fare-thee-weel, thou first and fairest!
Fare-thee-weel, thou best and dearest!
Thine be ilka joy and treasure,
Peace, Enjoyment, Love and Pleasure!

Ae fond kiss, and then we sever!
Ae fareweel, alas, for ever!
Deep in heart-wrung tears I'll pledge thee,
Warring sighs and groans I'll wage thee.

ae = one; *wage* = pledge; *nae* = no; *naething* =
nothing; *sae* = so; *ilka* = every.

My Luve Is Like a Red, Red Rose

Robert Burns

O, my Luve is like a red, red rose,
That's newly sprung in June;
O, my Luve is like the melodie
That's sweetly play'd in tune.

As fair art thou, my bonie lass,
So deep in luve am I;

And I will luve thee still, my Dear,
Till a' the seas gang dry.

Till a' the seas gang dry, my Dear,
And the rocks melt wi' the sun:
I will luve thee still, my Dear,
While the sands o' life shall run.

And fare thee weel, my only Luve!
And fare thee weel, a while!
And I will come again, my Luve,
Tho' it were ten thousand mile!

Burns created this poem from a number of old
Scottish ballads.
bonie = pretty; *a'* = all; *gang* = go; *weel* = well.
When reciting the poem, it may be better to omit
the 'O' in the first and third lines of the first verse.

Sweet Afton

Robert Burns

'Sweet Afton' is the Afton Water, a river in Ayrshire.
'Mary' is probably Mary Campbell, a girl Burns
addressed in another poem as 'Highland Mary'.

Flow gently, sweet Afton, among thy green braes,
Flow gently, I'll sing thee a song in thy praise;
My Mary's asleep by thy murmuring stream,
Flow gently, sweet Afton, disturb not her dream.

Thou stock dove whose echo resounds thro' the glen,
Ye wild whistling blackbirds in yon thorny den,
Thou green-crested lapwing, thy screaming forbear,
I charge you, disturb not my slumbering Fair.

How lofty, sweet Afton, thy neighbouring hills,
Far mark'd with the courses of clear, winding rills;
There daily I wander as noon rises high,
My flocks and my Mary's sweet cot in my eye.

How pleasant thy banks and green vallies below,
Where wild in the woodlands the primroses blow;
There oft, as mild ev'ning weeps over the lea,
The sweet-scented birk shades my Mary and me.

Thy crystal stream, Afton, how lovely it glides,
And winds by the cot where my Mary resides;
How wanton thy waters her snowy feet lave,
As, gathering sweet flowerets, she stems thy clear wave.

Flow gently, sweet Afton, among thy green braes,
Flow gently, sweet River, the theme of my lays;
My Mary's asleep by thy murmuring stream,
Flow gently, sweet Afton, disturb not her dream.

braes = slopes, hillsides; *yon* = that; *cot* = cottage;
birk = birch tree; *lave* = wash.

She Walks in Beauty

Lord Byron (1788–1824)

Lord Byron wrote this poem about Anne Wilmot, his cousin's wife, after seeing her wearing mourning clothes with dark spangles on her dress.

She walks in beauty, like the night
 Of cloudless climes and starry skies;
And all that's best of dark and bright
 Meet in her aspect and her eyes:
Thus mellow'd to that tender light
 Which heaven to gaudy day denies.

One shade the more, one ray the less,
 Had half impair'd the nameless grace
Which waves in every raven tress,
 Or softly lightens o'er her face;
Where thoughts serenely sweet express,
 How pure, how dear their dwelling-place.

And on that cheek, and o'er that brow,
 So soft, so calm, yet eloquent,
The smiles that win, the tints that glow,
 But tell of days in goodness spent,
A mind at peace with all below,
 A heart whose love is innocent!

Freedom and Love

Thomas Campbell (1777–1844)

Campbell was a Scottish poet and journalist. He was
elected rector of Glasgow University three times,
and helped establish the University of London.

How delicious is the winning
Of a kiss at love's beginning,
When two mutual hearts are sighing
For the knot there's no untying!

Yet remember, 'midst your wooing,
Love has bliss, but Love has ruing;
Other smiles may make you fickle,
Tears for other charms may trickle.

Love he comes, and Love he tarries,
Just as fate or fancy carries;
Longest stays, when sorest chidden;
Laughs and flies, when press'd and bidden.

Bind the sea to slumber stilly,
Bind its odour to the lily,
Bind the aspen ne'er to quiver,
Then bind Love to last for ever.

Love's a fire that needs renewal
Of fresh beauty for its fuel:
Love's wing moults when caged and captured,
Only free, he soars enraptured.

Can you keep the bee from ranging
Or the ringdove's neck from changing?
No! nor fetter'd Love from dying
In the knot there's no untying.

Jabberwocky

Lewis Carroll (1832–1898)

Lewis Carroll is the pen-name of Charles Dodgson, a mathematics lecturer at Oxford University. Carroll is famous for his nonsense verse, especially that found in *Alice's Adventures in Wonderland* and its sequel *Through the Looking-Glass and What Alice Found There*. This poem comes from *Through the Looking-Glass*.

'Twas brillig, and the slithy toves
  Did gyre and gimble in the wabe;
All mimsy were the borogoves,
  And the mome raths outgrabe.

'Beware the Jabberwock, my son!
  The jaws that bite, the claws that catch!
Beware the Jubjub bird, and shun
  The frumious Bandersnatch!'

He took his vorpal sword in hand:
  Long time the manxome foe he sought —
So rested he by the Tumtum tree,
  And stood awhile in thought.

And as in uffish thought he stood,
  The Jabberwock, with eyes of flame,
Came whiffling through the tulgey wood,
  And burbled as it came!

One, two! One, two! And through and through
  The vorpal blade went snicker-snack!
He left it dead, and with its head
  He went galumphing back.

'And hast thou slain the Jabberwock?
  Come to my arms, my beamish boy!
O frabjous day! Callooh! Callay!'
  He chortled in his joy.

'Twas brillig, and the slithy toves
  Did gyre and gimble in the wabe;
All mimsy were the borogoves,
  And the mome raths outgrabe.

In *Through the Looking-Glass*, Humpty Dumpty explains the meaning of some of the odd words in this poem to Alice. His explanations also suggest the correct pronunciations of the words:

'brillig' means four o'clock in the afternoon;
'slithy' means 'lithe and slimy';
'toves' are animals a bit like badgers, a bit like lizards, and a bit like corkscrews;
to 'gyre' is to go round and round like a gyroscope;
to 'gimble' is to make holes like a gimlet;
the 'wabe' is the plot of grass round a sun-dial;
'mimsy' is 'flimsy and miserable';
a 'borogove' is a thin, shabby-looking bird with all its feathers sticking out;
a 'rath' is a sort of green pig;
'mome' is possibly short for 'from home' – meaning that the raths had lost their way;
to 'outgrabe' is to produce something between a bellow and a whistle, with a sneeze in the middle.

The Walrus and the Carpenter

Lewis Carroll

This is another poem from *Through the Looking-Glass*, written in the style of a traditional English ballad. Some people have read anti-political or anti-religious views into this poem, but it is probably best just taken at face value as the nonsense it first seems to be.

The sun was shining on the sea,
    Shining with all his might:
He did his very best to make
    The billows smooth and bright —
And this was odd, because it was
    The middle of the night.

The moon was shining sulkily,
    Because she thought the sun
Had got no business to be there
    After the day was done —
'It's very rude of him,' she said,
    'To come and spoil the fun!'

The sea was wet as wet could be,
    The sands were dry as dry.
You could not see a cloud, because
    No cloud was in the sky:
No birds were flying overhead —
    There were no birds to fly.

The Walrus and the Carpenter
    Were walking close at hand.
They wept like anything to see
    Such quantities of sand:
'If this were only cleared away,'
    They said, 'it would be grand!'

'If seven maids with seven mops
    Swept it for half a year,
Do you suppose,' the Walrus said,
    'That they could get it clear?'
'I doubt it,' said the Carpenter,
    And shed a bitter tear.

'O Oysters, come and walk with us!'
    The Walrus did beseech.
'A pleasant walk, a pleasant talk,
    Along the briny beach:
We cannot do with more than four,
    To give a hand to each.'

The eldest Oyster looked at him,
    But never a word he said:

The eldest Oyster winked his eye,
    And shook his heavy head —
Meaning to say he did not choose
    To leave the oyster-bed.

But four young Oysters hurried up,
    All eager for the treat:
Their coats were brushed, their faces washed,
    Their shoes were clean and neat —
And this was odd, because, you know,
    They hadn't any feet.

Four other Oysters followed them,
    And yet another four;
And thick and fast they came at last,
    And more, and more, and more —
All hopping through the frothy waves,
    And scrambling to the shore.

The Walrus and the Carpenter
    Walked on a mile or so,
And then they rested on a rock
    Conveniently low;
And all the little Oysters stood
    And waited in a row.

'The time has come,' the Walrus said,
    'To talk of many things:
Of shoes — and ships — and sealing-wax —
    And cabbages — and kings —

And why the sea is boiling hot—
   And whether pigs have wings.'

'But wait a bit,' the Oysters cried,
   'Before we have our chat;
For some of us are out of breath,
   And all of us are fat!'
'No hurry!' said the Carpenter.
   They thanked him much for that.

'A loaf of bread,' the Walrus said,
   'Is what we chiefly need:
Pepper and vinegar besides
   Are very good indeed —
Now if you're ready, Oysters dear,
   We can begin to feed.'

'But not on us!' the Oysters cried,
   Turning a little blue.
'After such kindness, that would be
   A dismal thing to do!'
'The night is fine,' the Walrus said,
   'Do you admire the view?

'It was so kind of you to come!
   And you are very nice!'
The Carpenter said nothing but
   'Cut us another slice.
I wish you were not quite so deaf —
   I've had to ask you twice!'

'It seems a shame,' the Walrus said,
'To play them such a trick,
After we've brought them out so far,
And made them trot so quick!'
The Carpenter said nothing but
'The butter's spread too thick!'

'I weep for you,' the Walrus said;
'I deeply sympathize.'
With sobs and tears he sorted out
Those of the largest size,
Holding his pocket-handkerchief
Before his streaming eyes.

'O Oysters,' said the Carpenter,
'You've had a pleasant run!
Shall we be trotting home again?'
But answer came there none —
And this was scarcely odd, because
They'd eaten every one.

This is quite a long poem, but you will probably find
that you already know parts of it – for example,
the lines about 'shoes and ships and sealing-wax
and cabbages and kings' – which will make it easier
to learn. Visualizing the story will also help you
commit it to memory.

Gold Leaves

G K Chesterton (1874–1936)

Lo! I am come to autumn,
  When all the leaves are gold;
Grey hairs and golden leaves cry out
  The year and I are old.

In youth I sought the prince of men,
  Captain in cosmic wars,
Our Titan, even the weeds would show
  Defiant, to the stars.

But now a great thing in the street
  Seems any human nod,
Where shift in strange democracy
  The million masks of God.

In youth I sought the golden flower
  Hidden in wood or wold,
But I am come to autumn,
  When all the leaves are gold.

Kubla Khan

Samuel Taylor Coleridge (1772–1834)

> According to Coleridge, *Kubla Khan* is only a fragment of what would have been a much longer poem had he not been interrupted by a visitor while writing it down. Coleridge had dreamed the whole poem but after the visitor left was unable to remember the parts he had not already committed to paper.

In Xanadu did Kubla Khan
  A stately pleasure-dome decree:
Where Alph, the sacred river, ran
Through caverns measureless to man
  Down to a sunless sea.
So twice five miles of fertile ground
  With walls and towers were girdled round;
And there were gardens bright with sinuous rills,
Where blossomed many an incense-bearing tree;
And here were forests ancient as the hills,
Enfolding sunny spots of greenery.

But O, that deep romantic chasm which slanted
Down the green hill athwart a cedarn cover!
A savage place! as holy and enchanted
As e'er beneath a waning moon was haunted
By woman wailing for her demon-lover!
And from this chasm, with ceaseless turmoil seething,
As if this earth in fast thick pants were breathing,
A mighty fountain momently was forced;
Amid whose swift half-intermitted burst
Huge fragments vaulted like rebounding hail,
Or chaffy grain beneath the thresher's flail:
And mid these dancing rocks at once and ever
It flung up momently the sacred river.
Five miles meandering with a mazy motion
Through wood and dale the sacred river ran,
Then reached the caverns measureless to man,
And sank in tumult to a lifeless ocean;
And 'mid this tumult Kubla heard from far
Ancestral voices prophesying war!

The shadow of the dome of pleasure
   Floated midway on the waves;
   Where was heard the mingled measure
   From the fountain and the caves.
It was a miracle of rare device,
A sunny pleasure-dome with caves of ice!

   A damsel with a dulcimer
    In a vision once I saw:
   It was an Abyssinian maid,
    And on her dulcimer she played,
   Singing of Mount Abora.
   Could I revive within me
   Her symphony and song,
To such a deep delight 'twould win me,
That with music loud and long,
I would build that dome in air,
That sunny dome! those caves of ice!
And all who heard should see them there,
And all should cry, Beware! Beware!
His flashing eyes, his floating hair!
Weave a circle round him thrice,
   And close your eyes with holy dread
   For he on honey-dew hath fed,
And drunk the milk of Paradise.

Answer to a Child's Question

Samuel Taylor Coleridge

In 1795, Coleridge became friends with the poet William Wordsworth, and together they produced *Lyrical Ballads*, a book which marks the beginning of Romanticism in English poetry. Two aspects of Romanticism are its appreciation of the beauties of nature and the free expression of emotion. You can see both of these in this little poem, which may well have been based on Coleridge's answer to a young child's questioning.

Do you ask what the birds say? The Sparrow, the Dove,
The Linnet and Thrush say, 'I love and I love!'
In the winter they're silent — the wind is so strong;
What it says, I don't know, but it sings a loud song.
But green leaves, and blossoms, and sunny warm weather,
And singing, and loving — all come back together.
But the Lark is so brimful of gladness and love,
The green fields below him, the blue sky above,
That he sings, and he sings; and for ever sings he —
'I love my Love, and my Love loves me!'

Leisure

W H Davies (1871–1940)

William Henry Davies was born in Wales but emigrated to North America at the age of 22. There he lived as a tramp and casual worker until he lost a leg while jumping a train in Canada. He subsequently returned to England. Much of Davies' poetry shows his love of nature. *Leisure* is probably his best-known poem.

What is this life if, full of care,
We have no time to stand and stare?

No time to stand beneath the boughs
And stare as long as sheep or cows:

No time to see, when woods we pass,
Where squirrels hide their nuts in grass:

No time to see, in broad daylight,
Streams full of stars, like skies at night:

No time to turn at Beauty's glance,
And watch her feet, how they can dance:

No time to wait till her mouth can
Enrich that smile her eyes began?

A poor life this if, full of care,
We have no time to stand and stare.

The Cat

W H Davies

Within that porch, across the way,
  I see two naked eyes this night;
Two eyes that neither shut nor blink,
  Searching my face with a green light.

But cats to me are strange, so strange —
  I cannot sleep if one is near;
And though I'm sure I see those eyes,
  I'm not so sure a body's there!

The Kingfisher

W H Davies

It was the Rainbow gave thee birth,
  And left thee all her lovely hues;
And, as her mother's name was Tears,
  So runs it in my blood to choose
For haunts the lonely pools, and keep
In company with trees that weep.

Go you and, with such glorious hues,
  Live with proud Peacocks in green parks;
On lawns as smooth as shining glass,
  Let every feather show its marks;
Get thee on boughs and clap thy wings
Before the windows of proud kings.

Nay, lovely Bird, thou art not vain;
  Thou hast no proud, ambitious mind;
I also love a quiet place
  That's green, away from all mankind;
A lonely pool, and let a tree
Sigh with her bosom over me.

The Listeners

Walter de la Mare (1873–1956)

Walter de la Mare was an English poet and novelist.
This eerie poem leaves it to our own imaginations
to decide what the background to this episode
might be – who is the Traveller and why has he
come . . . and who are 'they'?

'Is there anybody there?' said the Traveller,
  Knocking on the moonlit door;
And his horse in the silence champed the grass
  Of the forest's ferny floor;
And a bird flew up out of the turret,
  Above the Traveller's head:
And he smote upon the door again a second time;
  'Is there anybody there?' he said.
But no one descended to the Traveller;
  No head from the leaf-fringed sill
Leaned over and looked into his grey eyes,
  Where he stood perplexed and still.
But only a host of phantom listeners
  That dwelt in the lone house then
Stood listening in the quiet of the moonlight
  To that voice from the world of men:
Stood thronging the faint moonbeams on the dark stair,
  That goes down to the empty hall,

Hearkening in an air stirred and shaken
   By the lonely Traveller's call.
And he felt in his heart their strangeness,
   Their stillness answering his cry,
While his horse moved, cropping the dark turf,
   'Neath the starred and leafy sky;
For he suddenly smote on the door, even
   Louder, and lifted his head: —
'Tell them I came, and no one answered,
   That I kept my word,' he said.
Never the least stir made the listeners,
   Though every word he spake
Fell echoing through the shadowiness of the still house
   From the one man left awake:
Ay, they heard his foot upon the stirrup,
   And the sound of iron on stone,
And how the silence surged softly backward,
   When the plunging hoofs were gone.

There are no breaks in this poem, but you will find it easy to memorize if you picture the parts of the story as it unfolds – the traveller knocking on the door (the first two lines), the horse eating the grass (the next two lines), the birds flying out of the turret (the next two lines) and so on. Keeping in mind the rhyme scheme of the poem will also help you commit it to memory.

Because I Could Not Stop for Death

Emily Dickinson (1830–1886)

Emily Dickinson was born in Amherst, Massachusetts. Though few of her poems were published in her lifetime, she was recognized as a 'new and original poetic genius' after her death. Her style, which deploys an idiosyncratic approach to punctuation, is one of beauty and vigour.

Because I could not stop for Death —
He kindly stopped for me —
The Carriage held but just Ourselves —
And Immortality.
We slowly drove — He knew no haste
And I had put away
My labor and my leisure too,
For His Civility —
We passed the School, where Children strove
At Recess — in the Ring —
We passed the Fields of Gazing Grain —
We passed the Setting Sun —
Or rather — He passed Us —
The Dews grew quivering and Chill —

For only Gossamer, my Gown —
My Tippet — only Tulle —
We paused before a House that seemed
A Swelling of the Ground —
The Roof was scarcely visible —
The Cornice — in the Ground —
Since then — 'tis Centuries — and yet
Feels shorter than the Day
I first surmised the Horses' Heads
Were toward Eternity —

Have You Got a Brook in Your Little Heart

Emily Dickinson

Have you got a Brook in your little heart,
Where bashful flowers blow,
And blushing birds go down to drink,
And shadows tremble so —

And nobody knows, so still it flows,
That any brook is there,
And yet your little draught of life
Is daily drunken there —

Why, look out for the little brook in March,
When the rivers overflow,
And the snows come hurrying from the hills,
And the bridges often go —

And later, in *August* it may be —
When the meadows parching lie,
Beware, lest this little brook of life,
Some burning noon go dry!

'Hope' is the Thing with Feathers

Emily Dickinson

'Hope' is the thing with feathers —
That perches in the soul —
And sings the tune without the words —
And never stops — at all —
And sweetest — in the Gale — is heard —
And sore must be the storm —
That could abash the little Bird
That kept so many warm —
I've heard it in the chillest land —
And on the strangest Sea —
Yet, never, in Extremity,
It asked a crumb of me.

If I Can Stop One Heart from Breaking

Emily Dickinson

If I can stop one heart from breaking
I shall not live in vain
If I can ease one life the aching
Or cool one pain
Or help one fainting robin
Unto his nest again
I shall not live in vain

The Morns Are Meeker Than They Were

Emily Dickinson

The morns are meeker than they were —
The nuts are getting brown —
The berry's cheek is plumper —
The Rose is out of town.

The Maple wears a gayer scarf —
The field a scarlet gown —
Lest I should seem old fashioned
I'll put a trinket on.

No Man Is an Island

John Donne (1572?–1631)

John Donne was an English poet and, in his later years, an Anglican priest. 'No Man Is an Island' is not strictly a poem, but part of a longer 'meditation' from his *Devotions upon Emergent Occasions*. However, it reads well as free verse and is often included in poetry collections.

No man is an island,
Entire of itself;
Every man is a piece of the Continent,
A part of the main.
If a clod be washed away by the sea,
Europe is the less
As well as if a promontory were
As well as if a manor of thy friend's
Or of thine own were:
Any man's death diminishes me,
Because I am involved in Mankind;
And therefore never send to know for whom the
    bell tolls;
It tolls for thee.

Holy Sonnet 10

John Donne

Death, be not proud, though some have called thee
  Mighty and dreadful, for thou art not so;
  For those whom thou think'st thou dost overthrow
Die not, poor Death, nor yet canst thou kill me.
From rest and sleep, which but thy pictures be,
  Much pleasure — then from thee much more must
  flow;
  And soonest our best men with thee do go,
Rest of their bones and soul's delivery.
Thou'rt slave to fate, chance, kings, and desperate men,
  And dost with poison, war, and sickness dwell;
  And poppy or charms can make us sleep as well
And better than thy stroke. Why swell'st thou then?
  One short sleep past, we wake eternally
  And death shall be no more. Death, thou shalt die.

Happy the Man

John Dryden (1631–1700)

> John Dryden was an English poet, and became
> Poet Laureate in 1668. Among his poetry are many
> excellent translations from Latin poets, and this is
> one of them, a translation of a poem from Horace's
> *Odes*. It is interesting to compare the feelings
> expressed here with those of William Ernest
> Henley's *Invictus* (see page 89).

Happy the man, and happy he alone,
   He who can call today his own:
   He who, secure within, can say,
Tomorrow do thy worst, for I have lived today.
   Be fair or foul or rain or shine
The joys I have possessed, in spite of fate, are mine.
Not Heaven itself upon the past has power,
But what has been, has been, and I have had my hour.

My Mind to Me a Kingdom Is

Sir Edward Dyer (1543–1607)

Sir Edward Dyer was a courtier at the court of
Queen Elizabeth I of England, and enjoyed some
reputation as a poet. He was considered to be a
man 'who would not stoop to fawn'.

My mind to me a kingdom is;
Such perfect joys therein I find,
That it excels all other bliss
That earth affords or grows by kind.
  Though much I want which most would have,
  Yet still my mind forbids to crave.

No princely pomp, no wealthy store,
No force to win the victory,
No wily wit to salve a sore,
No shape to feed a loving eye;
  To none of these I yield as thrall,
  For why? my mind doth serve for all.

I see how plenty suffers oft,
And hasty climbers soon do fall;
I see that those which are aloft
Mishap doth threaten most of all;
   They get with toil, they keep with fear;
   Such cares my mind could never bear.

Content I live, this is my stay;
I seek no more than may suffice;
I press to bear no haughty sway;
Look, what I lack my mind supplies.
   Lo, thus I triumph like a king,
   Content with that my mind doth bring.

Some have too much, yet still do crave
I little have, and seek no more:
They are but poor, though much they have
And I am rich with little store:
   They poor, I rich; they beg, I give;
   They lack, I leave; they pine, I live.

I laugh not at another's loss,
Nor grudge not at another's gain;
No worldly waves my mind can toss,
My state at one doth still remain.
   I fear no foe, I fawn no friend,
   I loathe not life, nor dread my end.

Some weigh their pleasure by their lust,
Their wisdom by their rage of will;
Their treasure is their only trust,
A cloakèd craft their store of skill;
  But all the pleasure that I find
  Is to maintain a quiet mind.

My wealth is health and perfect ease,
And conscience clear my chief defence;
I neither seek by bribes to please,
Nor by deceit to breed offence.
  Thus do I live, thus will I die;
  Would all did so as well as I!

There are eight stanzas in this poem, making 48
lines in all, which is quite manageable if taken a
stanza at a time. Here again, noting the rhyme
scheme will help you learn the poem.

On a Cat, Ageing

Sir Alexander Gray (1882–1968)

> Sir Alexander Gray was born in Dundee, Scotland, and became a professor of economics. He wrote poetry in English and translated German and Danish poetry into Scots.

He blinks upon the hearth-rug,
And yawns in deep content,
Accepting all the comforts
That Providence has sent.

Louder he purrs and louder,
In one glad hymn of praise
For all the night's adventures,
For quiet restful days.

Life will go on forever,
With all that cat can wish;
Warmth and the glad procession
Of fish and milk and fish.

Only — the thought disturbs him —
He's noticed once or twice,
The times are somehow breeding
A nimbler race of mice.

Old Furniture

Thomas Hardy (1840–1928)

> Thomas Hardy was an English novelist, dramatist and poet. Among his best-known novels are *Far from the Madding Crowd* and *Tess of the D'Urbervilles.*

I know not how it may be with others
  Who sit amid relics of householdry
That date from the days of their mothers' mothers,
  But well I know how it is with me
    Continually.

I see the hands of the generations
  That owned each shiny familiar thing
In play on its knobs and indentations,
  And with its ancient fashioning
    Still dallying:

Hands behind hands, growing paler and paler,
  As in a mirror a candle-flame
Shows images of itself, each frailer
  As it recedes, though the eye may frame
    Its shape the same.

On the clock's dull dial a foggy finger,
  Moving to set the minutes right
With tentative touches that lift and linger
  In the wont of a moth on a summer night,
    Creeps to my sight.

On this old viol, too, fingers are dancing —
  As whilom — just over the strings by the nut,
The tip of a bow receding, advancing
  In airy quivers, as if it would cut
    The plaintive gut.

And I see a face by that box for tinder,
  Glowing forth in fits from the dark,
And fading again, as the linten cinder
  Kindles to red at the flinty spark,
    Or goes out stark.

Well, well. It is best to be up and doing,
  The world has no use for one to-day
Who eyes things thus — no aim pursuing!
  He should not continue in this stay,
    But sink away.

Snow in the Suburbs

Thomas Hardy

Every branch big with it,
Bent every twig with it;
Every fork like a white web-foot;
Every street and pavement mute:
Some flakes have lost their way, and grope
back upward when
Meeting those meandering down they turn
and descend again.
The palings are glued together like a wall,
And there is no waft of wind with the
fleecy fall.

A sparrow enters the tree,
Whereon immediately
A snow-lump thrice his own slight size
Descends on him and showers his head
and eyes,
And overturns him,
And near inurns him,
And lights on a nether twig, when its
brush
Starts off a volley of other lodging lumps
with a rush.

The steps are a blanched slope,
Up which, with feeble hope,
A black cat comes, wide-eyed and thin;
And we take him in.

Inurn = entomb.

The Darkling Thrush

Thomas Hardy

I leant upon a coppice gate
When Frost was spectre-grey,
And Winter's dregs made desolate
The weakening eye of day.
The tangled bine-stems scored the sky
Like strings of broken lyres,
And all mankind that haunted nigh
Had sought their household fires.
The land's sharp features seemed to be
The Century's corpse outleant,

His crypt the cloudy canopy,
The wind his death-lament.
The ancient pulse of germ and birth
Was shrunken hard and dry,
And every spirit upon earth
Seemed fervourless as I.
At once a voice arose among
The bleak twigs overhead
In full-hearted evensong
Of joy illimited;
An agèd thrush, frail, gaunt, and small,
In blast-beruffled plume,
Had chosen thus to fling his soul
Upon the growing gloom.
So little cause for carolings
Of such ecstatic sound
Was written on terrestrial things
Afar or nigh around,
That I could think there trembled through
His happy good-night air
Some blessed Hope, whereof he knew
And I was unaware.

Darkling means 'in the dark'. (Poets are fond of this word – you will find it in other poems in this anthology.) Bine-stems are the stems of climbing plants such as hops.

The Oxen

Thomas Hardy

Christmas Eve, and twelve of the clock.
'Now they are all on their knees,'
An elder said as we sat in a flock
By the embers in hearthside ease.

We pictured the meek mild creatures where
They dwelt in their strawy pen,
Nor did it occur to one of us there
To doubt they were kneeling then.

So fair a fancy few would weave
In these years! Yet, I feel,
If someone said on Christmas Eve,
'Come; see the oxen kneel,

'In the lonely barton by yonder coomb
Our childhood used to know,'
I should go with him in the gloom,
Hoping it might be so.

A *barton* is a farmyard; a *coomb* is a valley or a
hollow in a hillside.

The Ruined Maid

Thomas Hardy

An amusing poem about a girl who has left the
countryside and made good – or gone bad,
depending on your point of view – in the town.
The two girls belong to Dorset, in the south-west
of England, as did Hardy. The dialect words Hardy
uses add to the characterization and are explained
at the end of the poem.

'O 'Melia, my dear, this does everything crown!
Who could have supposed I should meet you in Town?
And whence such fair garments, such prosperi-ty?' —
"O didn't you know I'd been ruined?" said she.

— 'You left us in tatters, without shoes or socks,
Tired of digging potatoes, and spudding up docks;
And now you've gay bracelets and bright feathers three!' —
"Yes: that's how we dress when we're ruined," said she.

— 'At home in the barton you said 'thee' and 'thou,'
And 'thik oon,' and 'theäs oon,' and 't'other'; but now
Your talking quite fits 'ee for high compa-ny!' —
"Some polish is gained with one's ruin," said she.

— 'Your hands were like paws then, your face blue and
    bleak
But now I'm bewitched by your delicate cheek,
And your little gloves fit as on any la-dy!' —
"We never do work when we're ruined," said she.

— 'You used to call home-life a hag-ridden dream,
And you'd sigh, and you'd sock; but at present you seem
To know not of megrims or melancho-ly!' —
"True. One's pretty lively when ruined," said she.

— 'I wish I had feathers, a fine sweeping gown,
And a delicate face, and could strut about Town!' —
"My dear — a raw country girl, such as you be,
Cannot quite expect that. You ain't ruined," said she.

> In the dialect of Dorset, *spudding up docks* =
> digging up weeds; *barton* = farmyard; *thik oon* =
> that one; *theäs oon* = this one; *t'other* = the other;
> *'ee* = you; *sock* = sulk; *megrims* = depression, low
> spirits.
>
> Notice how the rhythm and rhyme scheme of the
> poem require you to stress the syllables -ty, -ny, -dy
> and -ly.

Invictus

William Ernest Henley (1849–1903)

William Henley was an English poet, playwright and critic. He lost a leg to disease, but refused to allow doctors to remove his other leg, showing the courage and determination of his character that are reflected in the words of this poem. *Invictus* is Latin for 'undefeated'. Nelson Mandela recited this poem while in prison.

Out of the night that covers me,
    Black as the Pit from pole to pole,
I thank whatever gods may be
    For my unconquerable soul.
In the fell clutch of circumstance
    I have not winced nor cried aloud.
Under the bludgeoning of chance
    My head is bloody, but unbowed.
Beyond this place of wrath and tears
    Looms but the Horror of the shade,
And yet the menace of the years
    Finds, and shall find, me unafraid.
It matters not how strait the gate,
    How charged with punishments the scroll,
I am the master of my fate:
    I am the captain of my soul.

Loveliest of Trees, the Cherry Now

A E Housman (1859–1936)

Alfred Edward Housman was a distinguished classical scholar, professor of Latin first at University College, London, and then at Cambridge. But he is now better known for his poetry.

Loveliest of trees, the cherry now
Is hung with bloom along the bough,
And stands about the woodland ride
Wearing white for Eastertide.

Now, of my threescore years and ten,
Twenty will not come again,
And take from seventy springs a score,
It only leaves me fifty more.

And since to look at things in bloom
Fifty springs are little room,
About the woodlands I will go
To see the cherry hung with snow.

Because I Liked You Better

A E Housman

Because I liked you better
   Than suits a man to say,
It irked you, and I promised
   To throw the thought away.

To put the world between us
   We parted, stiff and dry;
'Good-bye,' said you, 'forget me.'
   'I will, no fear,' said I.

If here, where clover whitens
   The dead man's knoll, you pass,
And no tall flower to meet you
   Starts in the trefoiled grass,

Halt by the headstone naming
   The heart no longer stirred,
And say the lad that loved you
   Was one that kept his word.

Dreams

Langston Hughes (1902–1967)

Langston Hughes was an African-American poet, dramatist and novelist, a leading figure in the Harlem Renaissance of the 1920s and 1930s.

Hold fast to dreams
For if dreams die
Life is a broken-winged bird
That cannot fly.

Hold fast to dreams
For when dreams go
Life is a barren field
Frozen with snow.

Abou Ben Adhem

J H Leigh Hunt (1784–1859)

James Henry Leigh Hunt was an English essayist, poet and journalist and a friend of Keats and Shelley.

Abou Ben Adhem (may his tribe increase!)
Awoke one night from a deep dream of peace,
And saw, within the moonlight in his room,
Making it rich, and like a lily in bloom,
An angel writing in a book of gold:—
Exceeding peace had made Ben Adhem bold,
And to the Presence in the room he said,
 'What writest thou?' — The vision raised its head,
And with a look made of all sweet accord,
Answered, 'The names of those who love the Lord.'
'And is mine one?' said Abou. 'Nay, not so,'
Replied the angel. Abou spoke more low,
But cheerly still, and said, 'I pray thee, then,
Write me as one that loves his fellow men.'
 The angel wrote, and vanished. The next night
It came again with a great wakening light,
And showed the names whom love of God had blest,
And lo! Ben Adhem's name led all the rest.

Song at the Beginning of Autumn

Elizabeth Jennings (1926–2001)

Elizabeth Jennings was an English poet who lived most of her life in Oxford.

Now watch this autumn that arrives
In smells. All looks like summer still;
Colours are quite unchanged, the air
On green and white serenely thrives.
Heavy the trees with growth and full
The fields. Flowers flourish everywhere.

Proust who collected time within
A child's cake would understand
The ambiguity of this —
Summer still raging while a thin
Column of smoke stirs from the land
Proving that autumn gropes for us.

But every season is a kind
Of rich nostalgia. We give names —
Autumn and summer, winter, spring —
As though to unfasten from the mind
Our moods and give them outward forms.
We want the certain, solid thing.

But I am carried back against
My will into a childhood where
Autumn is bonfires, marbles, smoke;
I lean against my window fenced
From evocations in the air.
When I said autumn, autumn broke.

The reference to Proust and a cake relates to an
incident in Marcel Proust's novel *Du Côté de chez
Swann* in which the taste of a madeleine cake
dipped in tea revives in the narrator unexpected
forgotten memories of his childhood.

To Celia

Ben Jonson (1572–1637)

Ben Jonson was an English dramatist, poet and critic, regarded by many as second in importance only to Shakespeare. This poem comes from his play *Volpone*.

Drink to me only with thine eyes,
  And I will pledge with mine;
Or leave a kiss but in the cup
  And I'll not look for wine.
The thirst that from the soul doth rise
  Doth ask a drink divine;
But might I of Jove's nectar sup,
  I would not change for thine.

I sent thee late a rosy wreath,
  Not so much honouring thee
As giving it a hope that there
  It could not withered be;
But thou thereon didst only breathe,
  And sent'st it back to me;
Since when it grows, and smells, I swear,
  Not of itself but thee!

Warning

Jenny Joseph (1932–)

Jenny Joseph is an English poet. Her poem *Warning* has twice been voted the UK's most popular post-war poem, and the mention of the 'red hat' in the second line of the poem has given rise to an international women's organization, the Red Hat Society.

When I am an old woman I shall wear purple
With a red hat that doesn't go, and doesn't suit me,
And I shall spend my pension on brandy and summer
   gloves
And satin sandals, and say we've no money for butter.
I shall sit down on the pavement when I'm tired,
And gobble up samples in shops and press alarm bells
And run my stick along the public railings
And make up for the sobriety of my youth.
I shall go out in my slippers in the rain
And pick the flowers in other people's gardens,
And learn to spit.

You can wear terrible shirts and grow more fat
And eat three pounds of sausages at a go
Or only bread and pickle for a week
And hoard pens and pencils and beermats and things in
	boxes.

But now we must have clothes that keep us dry
And pay our rent and not swear in the street
And set a good example for the children.
We will have friends to dinner and read the papers.

But maybe I ought to practise a little now?
So people who know me are not too shocked and
	surprised
When suddenly I am old and start to wear purple.

La Belle Dame Sans Merci

John Keats (1795–1821)

As can be seen from his dates, Keats' life was short. He died of tuberculosis in Rome, in relative obscurity. However, his reputation grew throughout the 19th century and the house in which he died is now a 'must-see' for anyone who appreciates English poetry.

The first three poems in this group of five are quite long, but well worth committing to memory.

O what can ail thee knight at arms
Alone and palely loitering?
The sedge has withered from the lake
And no birds sing!

O what can ail thee knight at arms
So haggard and so woe begone?
The squirrel's granary is full
And the harvest's done.

I see a lily on thy brow
With anguish moist and fever dew,
And on thy cheeks a fading rose
Fast withereth too —

I met a lady in the meads
Full beautiful, a faery's child;
Her hair was long, her foot was light
And her eyes were wild —

I made a garland for her head,
And bracelets too, and fragrant zone:
She look'd at me as she did love
And made sweet moan —

I set her on my pacing steed
And nothing else saw all day long
For sidelong would she bend and sing
A faery's song —

She found me roots of relish sweet
And honey wild and manna dew
And sure in language strange she said
'I love thee true — '

She took me to her elfin grot,
And there she wept and sigh'd full sore
And there I shut her wild, wild eyes
With kisses four.

And there she lulled me asleep
And there I dream'd — Ah! woe betide!
The latest dream I ever dreamt
On the cold hill's side.

I saw pale kings and princes too
Pale warriors, death pale were they all;
They cried 'La belle dame sans merci
Hath thee in thrall!'

I saw their starv'd lips in the gloam
With horrid warning gaped wide
And I awoke and found me here
On the cold hill's side.

And this is why I sojourn here
Alone and palely loitering;
Though the sedge is wither'd from the lake,
And no birds sing.

Ode to a Nightingale

John Keats

My heart aches, and a drowsy numbness pains
  My sense, as though of hemlock I had drunk,
Or emptied some dull opiate to the drains
  One minute past, and Lethe-wards had sunk:
'Tis not through envy of thy happy lot,
  But being too happy in thine happiness,
   That thou, light-wingèd Dryad of the trees,
    In some melodious plot
  Of beechen green, and shadows numberless,
   Singest of summer in full-throated ease.

O, for a draught of vintage! that hath been
  Cool'd a long age in the deep-delvèd earth,
Tasting of Flora and the country-green,
  Dance, and Provençal song, and sunburnt mirth!
O for a beaker full of the warm South!
  Full of the true, the blushful Hippocrene,
   With beaded bubbles winking at the brim,
    And purple-stainèd mouth;
  That I might drink, and leave the world unseen,
   And with thee fade away into the forest dim:

Fade far away, dissolve, and quite forget
    What thou among the leaves hast never known,
The weariness, the fever, and the fret
    Here, where men sit and hear each other groan;
Where palsy shakes a few, sad, last grey hairs,
    Where youth grows pale, and spectre-thin, and dies;
        Where but to think is to be full of sorrow
            And leaden-eyed despairs;
    Where beauty cannot keep her lustrous eyes,
        Or new Love pine at them beyond to-morrow.

Away! away! for I will fly to thee,
    Not charioted by Bacchus and his pards,
But on the viewless wings of Poesy,
    Though the dull brain perplexes and retards:
Already with thee! tender is the night,
    And haply the Queen-Moon is on her throne,
        Cluster'd around by all her starry Fays;
            But here there is no light,
        Save what from heaven is with the breezes blown
            Through verdurous glooms and winding mossy ways.

I cannot see what flowers are at my feet,
    Nor what soft incense hangs upon the boughs,
But, in embalmèd darkness, guess each sweet
    Wherewith the seasonable month endows
The grass, the thicket, and the fruit-tree wild;

White hawthorn, and the pastoral eglantine;
  Fast fading violets cover'd up in leaves;
    And mid-May's eldest child,
  The coming musk-rose, full of dewy wine,
    The murmurous haunt of flies on summer eves.

Darkling I listen; and for many a time
  I have been half in love with easeful Death,
Call'd him soft names in many a musèd rhyme,
  To take into the air my quiet breath;
Now more than ever seems it rich to die,
    To cease upon the midnight with no pain,
    While thou art pouring forth thy soul abroad
      In such an ecstasy!
    Still wouldst thou sing, and I have ears in vain —
    To thy high requiem become a sod.

Thou wast not born for death, immortal Bird!
  No hungry generations tread thee down;
The voice I hear this passing night was heard
  In ancient days by emperor and clown:
Perhaps the self-same song that found a path
    Through the sad heart of Ruth, when, sick for home,
    She stood in tears amid the alien corn;
      The same that oft-times hath
    Charm'd magic casements, opening on the foam
Of perilous seas, in faery lands forlorn.

Forlorn! the very word is like a bell
  To toll me back from thee to my sole self.
Adieu! the fancy cannot cheat so well
  As she is fam'd to do, deceiving elf.
Adieu! adieu! thy plaintive anthem fades
  Past the near meadows, over the still stream,
    Up the hill-side; and now 'tis buried deep
      In the next valley-glades:
    Was it a vision, or a waking dream?
Fled is that music: — do I wake or sleep?

With eight ten-line stanzas, literary and Classical allusions and rather poetic language, this is perhaps not an easy poem to memorize, but it is well worth the effort. The key here is, as with all long poems, not to rush at it, but to tackle it patiently a line or two at a time, stanza by stanza. Keep practising what you have learned as you commit more and more of it to memory.

'Lethe' is in Greek mythology a river in the underworld, causing forgetfulness in anyone who drank its water; a 'dryad' is a tree-spirit, a nymph of the woods; 'Hippocrene' in Greek mythology is a fountain sacred to Apollo and the Muses; 'Bacchus' is the Roman god of wine; 'pards' are leopards. The reference to Ruth 'amid the alien corn' relates to the story of Ruth in the Bible.

To Autumn

John Keats

Season of mists and mellow fruitfulness,
  Close bosom-friend of the maturing sun;
Conspiring with him how to load and bless
  With fruit the vines that round the thatch-eaves run;
To bend with apples the moss'd cottage-trees,
  And fill all fruit with ripeness to the core;
    To swell the gourd, and plump the hazel shells
  With a sweet kernel; to set budding more,
And still more, later flowers for the bees,
Until they think warm days will never cease,
    For Summer has o'er-brimm'd their clammy cells.

Who hath not seen thee oft amid thy store?
  Sometimes whoever seeks abroad may find
Thee sitting careless on a granary floor,
  Thy hair soft-lifted by the winnowing wind;
Or on a half-reap'd furrow sound asleep,
  Drows'd with the fume of poppies, while thy hook
    Spares the next swath and all its twinèd flowers:
And sometimes like a gleaner thou dost keep
  Steady thy laden head across a brook;
  Or by a cider-press, with patient look,
    Thou watchest the last oozings, hours by hours.

Where are the songs of Spring? Ay, where are they?
  Think not of them, thou hast thy music too, —
    While barrèd clouds bloom the soft-dying day,
And touch the stubble-plains with rosy hue;
  Then in a wailful choir the small gnats mourn
  Among the river sallows, borne aloft
    Or sinking as the light wind lives or dies;
And full-grown lambs loud bleat from hilly bourn;
  Hedge-crickets sing; and now with treble soft
  The redbreast whistles from a garden-croft;
    And gathering swallows twitter in the skies.

'Redbreast' = the European robin.

O Solitude! If I Must with Thee Dwell

John Keats

O Solitude! if I must with thee dwell,
Let it not be among the jumbled heap
Of murky buildings: climb with me the steep, —
Nature's observatory — whence the dell,
In flowery slopes, its river's crystal swell,
May seem a span; let me thy vigils keep
'Mongst boughs pavilion'd, where the deer's swift leap
Startles the wild bee from the foxglove bell.
But though I'll gladly trace these scenes with thee,
Yet the sweet converse of an innocent mind,
Whose words are images of thoughts refined,
Is my soul's pleasure; and it sure must be
Almost the highest bliss of human-kind,
When to thy haunts two kindred spirits flee.

The Human Seasons

John Keats

Four Seasons fill the measure of the year;
  There are four seasons in the mind of man:
He has his lusty Spring, when fancy clear
Takes in all beauty with an easy span:
He has his Summer, when luxuriously
  Spring's honey'd cud of youthful thought he loves
To ruminate, and by such dreaming high
  Is nearest unto Heaven: quiet coves
His soul has in its Autumn, when his wings
  He furleth close; contented so to look
On mists in idleness — to let fair things
  Pass by unheeded as a threshold brook.
He has his Winter too of pale misfeature,
Or else he would forego his mortal nature.

Trees

Joyce Kilmer (1886–1918)

 Joyce Kilmer was an American writer and poet. He died in France during World War I.

I think that I shall never see
A poem lovely as a tree.

A tree whose hungry mouth is prest
Against the earth's sweet flowing breast;

A tree that looks at God all day,
And lifts her leafy arms to pray;

A tree that may in Summer wear
A nest of robins in her hair;

Upon whose bosom snow has lain;
Who intimately lives with rain.

Poems are made by fools like me,
But only God can make a tree.

If —

Rudyard Kipling (1865–1936)

Rudyard Kipling was an English writer and poet, born in Mumbai, India. He was famous for his stories and poems about British soldiers during the days of Empire, and for children's stories such as *The Jungle Book*. He was awarded the Nobel Prize for Literature in 1907.

If you can keep your head when all about you
  Are losing theirs and blaming it on you;
If you can trust yourself when all men doubt you,
  But make allowance for their doubting too:
If you can wait and not be tired by waiting,
  Or, being lied about, don't deal in lies,
Or being hated, don't give way to hating,
  And yet don't look too good, nor talk too wise:

If you can dream — and not make dreams your master;
  If you can think — and not make thoughts your aim;
If you can meet with Triumph and Disaster
  And treat those two impostors just the same;
If you can bear to hear the truth you've spoken
  Twisted by knaves to make a trap for fools,
Or watch the things you gave your life to, broken,
  And stoop and build 'em up with worn-out tools:

If you can make one heap of all your winnings
   And risk it on one turn of pitch-and-toss,
And lose, and start again at your beginnings,
   And never breathe a word about your loss;
If you can force your heart and nerve and sinew
   To serve your turn long after they are gone,
And so hold on when there is nothing in you
   Except the Will which says to them: 'Hold on!'

If you can talk with crowds and keep your virtue,
   Or walk with Kings — nor lose the common touch;
If neither foes nor loving friends can hurt you,
   If all men count with you, but none too much;
If you can fill the unforgiving minute
   With sixty seconds' worth of distance run,
Yours is the Earth and everything that's in it,
   And — which is more — you'll be a Man, my son!

I Keep Six Honest Serving-men

Rudyard Kipling

I keep six honest serving-men
   (They taught me all I knew);
Their names are What and Why and When
   And How and Where and Who.
I send them over land and sea,
   I send them east and west;
But after they have worked for me,
   I give them all a rest.

I let them rest from nine till five,
   For I am busy then,
As well as breakfast, lunch, and tea,
   For they are hungry men.
But different folk have different views;
   I know a person small —
She keeps ten million serving-men,
   Who get no rest at all!

She sends 'em abroad on her own affairs,
   From the second she opens her eyes —
One million Hows, two million Wheres,
   And seven million Whys!

Four-Feet (The Woman in His Life)

Rudyard Kipling

> This is a poem that will speak to everyone who has lost a beloved pet.

I have done mostly what most men do,
And pushed it out of my mind;
But I can't forget, if I wanted to,
Four-Feet trotting behind.

Day after day, the whole day through —
Wherever my road inclined —
Four-Feet said, 'I am coming with you!'
And trotted along behind.

Now I must go by some other round —
Which I shall never find —
Somewhere that does not carry the sound
Of Four-Feet trotting behind.

Change

Raymond Knister (1899–1932)

> Raymond Knister was a Canadian poet, novelist and
> story writer, born in what is now Lakeshore, Ontario.
> He drowned in a swimming accident in Lake St Clair.
> This poem is inscribed on his gravestone.

I shall not wonder more, then,
But I shall know.

Leaves change, and birds, flowers,
And after years are still the same.

The sea's breast heaves in sighs to the moon,
But they are moon and sea forever.

As in other times the trees stand tense and lonely,
And spread a hollow moan of other times.

You will be you yourself,
I'll find you more, not else,
For vintage of the woeful years.

The sea breathes, or broods, or loudens,
Is bright or is mist and the end of the world;
And the sea is constant to change.

I shall not wonder more, then,
But I shall know.

Beautiful Old Age

D H Lawrence (1885–1930)

D H Lawrence was an English poet and novelist, best known for his novels *Lady Chatterley's Lover*, *Women in Love* and *Sons and Lovers*, although many people believe his poems represent his best writing.

It ought to be lovely to be old
to be full of the peace that comes of experience
and wrinkled ripe fulfilment.

The wrinkled smile of completeness that follows a life
lived undaunted and unsoured with accepted lies.
If people lived without accepting lies
they would ripen like apples, and be scented like pippins
in their old age.

Soothing, old people should be, like apples
when one is tired of love.
Fragrant like yellowing leaves, and dim with the soft
stillness and satisfaction of autumn.

And a girl should say:
It must be wonderful to live and grow old.
Look at my mother, how rich and still she is! —

And a young man should think: By Jove
my father has faced all weathers, but it's been a life! —

Piano

D H Lawrence

Softly, in the dusk, a woman is singing to me;
Taking me back down the vista of years, till I see
A child sitting under the piano, in the boom of the
    tingling strings
And pressing the small, poised feet of a mother who
    smiles as she sings.
In spite of myself, the insidious mastery of song
Betrays me back, till the heart of me weeps to belong
To the old Sunday evenings at home, with winter outside
And hymns in the cosy parlour, the tinkling piano our
    guide.
So now it is vain for the singer to burst into clamour
With the great black piano appassionato. The glamour
Of childish days is upon me, my manhood is cast
Down in the flood of remembrance, I weep like a child
    for the past.

The Owl and the Pussy-cat

Edward Lear (1812–1888)

Edward Lear was an English artist and humorist whose nonsense verse has delighted readers young and old for more than 150 years. *The Owl and the Pussy-cat* is probably the best-known of his poems.

The Owl and the Pussy-cat went to sea
  In a beautiful pea-green boat,
They took some honey, and plenty of money,
  Wrapped up in a five-pound note.
The Owl looked up to the stars above,
  And sang to a small guitar,
'O lovely Pussy! O Pussy, my love,
  What a beautiful Pussy you are,
    You are,
    You are!
  What a beautiful Pussy you are!'

Pussy said to the Owl 'You elegant fowl!
  How charmingly sweet you sing!
O let us be married! too long we have tarried:
  But what shall we do for a ring?'
They sailed away, for a year and a day,
  To the land where the Bong-tree grows,
And there in a wood a Piggy-wig stood
  With a ring at the end of his nose,
    His nose,
    His nose,
  With a ring at the end of his nose.

'Dear Pig, are you willing to sell for one shilling
  Your ring?' Said the Piggy, 'I will.'
So they took it away, and were married next day
  By the Turkey who lives on the hill.
They dined on mince, and slices of quince,
  Which they ate with a runcible spoon;
And hand in hand, on the edge of the sand.
  They danced by the light of the moon,
    The moon,
    The moon,
  They danced by the light of the moon.

The Pobble Who Has No Toes

Edward Lear

The Pobble who has no toes
  Had once as many as we;
When they said, 'Some day you may lose them all;' —
  He replied, — 'Fish, fiddle-de-dee!'
And his Aunt Jobiska made him drink
Lavender water tinged with pink,
For she said, 'The World in general knows
There's nothing so good for a Pobble's toes!'

The Pobble who has no toes
  Swam across the Bristol Channel;
But before he set out he wrapped his nose
  In a piece of scarlet flannel.
For his Aunt Jobiska said 'No harm
Can come to his toes if his nose is warm;
And it's perfectly known that a Pobble's toes
Are safe, — provided he minds his nose.'

The Pobble swam fast and well,
  And when boats or ships came near him,
He tinkledy-binkledy-winkled a bell,
  So that all the world could hear him.
And all the Sailors and Admirals cried,

When they saw him nearing the further side, —
'He has gone to fish for his Aunt Jobiska's
Runcible Cat with crimson whiskers!'

But before he touched the shore,
  The shore of the Bristol Channel,
A sea-green porpoise carried away
  His wrapper of scarlet flannel.
And when he came to observe his feet,
Formerly garnished with toes so neat,
His face at once became forlorn,
On perceiving that all his toes were gone!

And nobody ever knew
  From that dark day to the present,
Whoso had taken the Pobble's toes,
  In a manner so far from pleasant.
Whether the shrimps, or crawfish gray,
Or crafty Mermaids stole them away —
Nobody knew; and nobody knows
How the Pobble was robbed of his twice five toes!

The Pobble who has no toes
  Was placed in a friendly Bark,
And they rowed him back, and carried him up
  To his Aunt Jobiska's Park.
And she made him a feast at his earnest wish
Of eggs and buttercups fried with fish; —
And she said, — 'It's a fact the whole world knows,
That Pobbles are happier without their toes.'

I Meant to Do My Work Today

Richard Le Gallienne (1866–1947)

Richard Le Gallienne (the name is stressed on the last syllable) was an English writer, journalist and poet.

I meant to do my work today —
　　But a brown bird sang in the apple tree,
And a butterfly flitted across the field,
　　And all the leaves were calling me.

And the wind went sighing over the land,
　　Tossing the grasses to and fro,
And a rainbow held out its shining hand —
　　So what could I do but laugh and go?

Excelsior

Henry Wadsworth Longfellow (1807–1882)

> Henry Wadsworth Longfellow was one of the most popular American poets of the 19th century, and *Excelsior* is one of his best-known poems.

The shades of night were falling fast,
As through an Alpine village passed
A youth, who bore, 'mid snow and ice,
A banner with the strange device,
　　Excelsior!

His brow was sad; his eye beneath,
Flashed like a falchion from its sheath,
And like a silver clarion rung
The accents of that unknown tongue,
　　Excelsior!

In happy homes he saw the light
Of household fires gleam warm and bright;
Above, the spectral glaciers shone,
And from his lips escaped a groan,
　　Excelsior!

'Try not the Pass!' the old man said;
'Dark lowers the tempest overhead,
The roaring torrent is deep and wide!'
And loud that clarion voice replied,
    Excelsior!

'Oh stay,' the maiden said, 'and rest
Thy weary head upon this breast!'
A tear stood in his bright blue eye,
But still he answered, with a sigh,
    Excelsior!

'Beware the pine-tree's withered branch!
Beware the awful avalanche!'
This was the peasant's last Good-night,
A voice replied, far up the height,
    Excelsior!

At break of day, as heavenward
The pious monks of Saint Bernard
Uttered the oft-repeated prayer,
A voice cried through the startled air,
    Excelsior!

A traveller, by the faithful hound,
Half-buried in the snow was found,
Still grasping in his hand of ice
That banner with the strange device,
Excelsior!

There in the twilight cold and gray,
Lifeless, but beautiful, he lay,
And from the sky, serene and far,
A voice fell, like a falling star,
Excelsior!

In Latin, 'excelsior' means 'higher still'. As Longfellow explained to an inquirer, this poem depicts a man who – in spite of temptations, fears, advice and warnings – presses on to accomplish his goal in life. The Alpine village represents 'the rough, cold paths of the world', the glaciers the man's fate. But at the end we are assured that, even after death, he will progress 'excelsior'.

A falchion, pronounced 'fawl-chon', is a type of short, curved sword.

Hiawatha's Childhood

Henry Wadsworth Longfellow

This excerpt from the long poem *The Song of Hiawatha* recounts the childhood of the Native American folk-hero Hiawatha, who was brought up by his grandmother Nokomis. Gitche Gumee, the 'Big-Sea-Water', is Lake Superior.

By the shores of Gitche Gumee,
By the shining Big-Sea-Water,
Stood the wigwam of Nokomis,
Daughter of the Moon, Nokomis.
Dark behind it rose the forest,
Rose the black and gloomy pine-trees,
Rose the firs with cones upon them;
Bright before it beat the water,
Beat the clear and sunny water,
Beat the shining Big-Sea-Water.
    There the wrinkled old Nokomis
Nursed the little Hiawatha,
Rocked him in his linden cradle,
Bedded soft in moss and rushes,
Safely bound with reindeer sinews;
Stilled his fretful wail by saying,
'Hush! the Naked Bear will hear thee!'
Lulled him into slumber, singing,

'Ewa-yea! my little owlet!
Who is this, that lights the wigwam?
With his great eyes lights the wigwam?
Ewa-yea! my little owlet!'
   Many things Nokomis taught him
Of the stars that shine in heaven;
Showed him Ishkoodah, the comet,
Ishkoodah, with fiery tresses,
Showed the Death-Dance of the spirits,
Warriors with their plumes and war-clubs
Flaring far away to northward
In the frosty nights of Winter;
Showed the broad white road in heaven,
Pathway of the ghosts, the shadows,
Running straight across the heavens,
Crowded with the ghosts, the shadows.
   At the door on summer evenings,
Sat the little Hiawatha;
Heard the whispering of the pine-trees,
Heard the lapping of the waters,
Sounds of music, words of wonder;
'Minne-wawa!' said the pine-trees,
'Mudway-aushka!' said the water.
   Saw the fire-fly Wah-wah-taysee,
Flitting through the dusk of evening,
With the twinkle of its candle
Lighting up the brakes and bushes,
And he sang the song of children,
Sang the song Nokomis taught him:
'Wah-wah-taysee, little fire-fly,

Little, flitting, white-fire insect,
Little, dancing, white-fire creature,
Light me with your little candle,
Ere upon my bed I lay me,
Ere in sleep I close my eyelids!'
   Saw the moon rise from the water,
Rippling, rounding from the water,
Saw the flecks and shadows on it,
Whispered, 'What is that, Nokomis?'
And the good Nokomis answered:
'Once a warrior, very angry,
Seized his grandmother, and threw her
Up into the sky at midnight;
Right against the moon he threw her;
'T is her body that you see there.'
   Saw the rainbow in the heaven,
In the eastern sky the rainbow,
Whispered, 'What is that, Nokomis?'
And the good Nokomis answered:
''T is the heaven of flowers you see there;
All the wild-flowers of the forest,
All the lilies of the prairie,
When on earth they fade and perish,
Blossom in that heaven above us.'
   When he heard the owls at midnight,
Hooting, laughing in the forest,
'What is that?' he cried in terror;
'What is that,' he said, 'Nokomis?'
And the good Nokomis answered:
'That is but the owl and owlet,

Talking in their native language,
Talking, scolding at each other.'
  Then the little Hiawatha
Learned of every bird its language,
Learned their names and all their secrets,
How they built their nests in Summer,
Where they hid themselves in Winter,
Talked with them whene'er he met them,
Called them 'Hiawatha's Chickens.'
  Of all beasts he learned the language,
Learned their names and all their secrets,
How the beavers built their lodges,
Where the squirrels hid their acorns,
How the reindeer ran so swiftly,
Why the rabbit was so timid,
Talked with them whene'er he met them,
Called them 'Hiawatha's Brothers.'

Notice how the regular rhythm and repetition
of similar lines in this poem drive it along. Let
the rhythm help you with the pronunciation of
unfamiliar names, such as Gitche Gumee.
  When learning the poem, pick out separate
episodes and learn each one as a unit before
moving on to the next.

Paul Revere's Ride

Henry Wadsworth Longfellow

> Another of Longfellow's well-known works, this
> poem records the ride of Boston silversmith Paul
> Revere in April 1775 to warn the American colonists
> of the approach of British troops. The ensuing
> battle at Lexington marked the beginning of the
> American War of Independence.

Listen, my children, and you shall hear
Of the midnight ride of Paul Revere,
On the eighteenth of April, in Seventy-five;
Hardly a man is now alive
Who remembers that famous day and year.

He said to his friend, 'If the British march
By land or sea from the town to-night,
Hang a lantern aloft in the belfry arch
Of the North Church tower as a signal light, —
One, if by land, and two, if by sea;
And I on the opposite shore will be,
Ready to ride and spread the alarm
Through every Middlesex village and farm,
For the country folk to be up and to arm.'

Then he said 'Good-night!' and with muffled oar
Silently rowed to the Charlestown shore,
Just as the moon rose over the bay,
Where swinging wide at her moorings lay
The Somerset, British man-of-war;
A phantom ship, with each mast and spar
Across the moon like a prison bar,
And a huge black hulk, that was magnified
By its own reflection in the tide.

Meanwhile, his friend, through alley and street,
Wanders and watches, with eager ears,
Till in the silence around him he hears
The muster of men at the barrack door,
The sound of arms, and the tramp of feet,
And the measured tread of the grenadiers,
Marching down to their boats on the shore.

Then he climbed the tower of the Old North Church,
By the wooden stairs, with stealthy tread,
To the belfry-chamber overhead,
And startled the pigeons from their perch
On the sombre rafters, that round him made
Masses and moving shapes of shade, —
By the trembling ladder, steep and tall,
To the highest window in the wall,
Where he paused to listen and look down
A moment on the roofs of the town
And the moonlight flowing over all.

Beneath, in the churchyard, lay the dead,
In their night-encampment on the hill,
Wrapped in silence so deep and still
That he could hear, like a sentinel's tread,
The watchful night-wind, as it went
Creeping along from tent to tent,
And seeming to whisper, 'All is well!'
A moment only he feels the spell
Of the place and the hour, and the secret dread
Of the lonely belfry and the dead;
For suddenly all his thoughts are bent
On a shadowy something far away,
Where the river widens to meet the bay, —
A line of black that bends and floats
On the rising tide, like a bridge of boats.

Meanwhile, impatient to mount and ride,
Booted and spurred, with a heavy stride
On the opposite shore walked Paul Revere.
Now he patted his horse's side,
Now he gazed at the landscape far and near,
Then, impetuous, stamped the earth,
And turned and tightened his saddle girth;
But mostly he watched with eager search

The belfry-tower of the Old North Church,
As it rose above the graves on the hill,
Lonely and spectral and sombre and still.
And lo! as he looks, on the belfry's height
A glimmer, and then a gleam of light!
He springs to the saddle, the bridle he turns,
But lingers and gazes, till full on his sight
A second lamp in the belfry burns!

A hurry of hoofs in a village street,
A shape in the moonlight, a bulk in the dark,
And beneath, from the pebbles, in passing, a spark
Struck out by a steed flying fearless and fleet;
That was all! And yet, through the gloom and the light,
The fate of a nation was riding that night;
And the spark struck out by that steed, in his flight,
Kindled the land into flame with its heat.

He has left the village and mounted the steep,
And beneath him, tranquil and broad and deep,
Is the Mystic, meeting the ocean tides;
And under the alders that skirt its edge,
Now soft on the sand, now loud on the ledge,
Is heard the tramp of his steed as he rides.

It was twelve by the village clock
When he crossed the bridge into Medford town.
He heard the crowing of the cock,
And the barking of the farmer's dog,
And felt the damp of the river fog,
That rises after the sun goes down.

It was one by the village clock,
When he galloped into Lexington.
He saw the gilded weathercock
Swim in the moonlight as he passed,
And the meeting-house windows, blank and bare,
Gaze at him with a spectral glare,
As if they already stood aghast
At the bloody work they would look upon.

It was two by the village clock,
When he came to the bridge in Concord town.
He heard the bleating of the flock,
And the twitter of birds among the trees,
And felt the breath of the morning breeze
Blowing over the meadow brown.
And one was safe and asleep in his bed
Who at the bridge would be first to fall,
Who that day would be lying dead,
Pierced by a British musket-ball.

You know the rest. In the books you have read
How the British Regulars fired and fled,
How the farmers gave them ball for ball,
From behind each fence and farm-yard wall,
Chasing the red-coats down the lane,
Then crossing the fields to emerge again
Under the trees at the turn of the road,
And only pausing to fire and load.

So through the night rode Paul Revere;
And so through the night went his cry of alarm
To every Middlesex village and farm, —
A cry of defiance and not of fear,
A voice in the darkness, a knock at the door,
And a word that shall echo forevermore!
For, borne on the night-wind of the Past,
Through all our history, to the last,
In the hour of darkness and peril and need,
The people will waken and listen to hear
The hurrying hoof-beats of that steed,
And the midnight message of Paul Revere.

This is one of the longer poems in the anthology,
but the story is well-known and the poem carries
us along easily, so it is not as hard to learn as you
might think.

The Three Kings

Henry Wadsworth Longfellow

This is Longfellow's telling of the Christmas story of the journey of the Magi to see the new-born Jesus in the stable in Bethlehem.

Three Kings came riding from far away,
   Melchior and Gaspar and Baltasar;
Three Wise Men out of the East were they,
And they travelled by night and they slept by day,
   For their guide was a beautiful, wonderful star.

The star was so beautiful, large, and clear,
   That all the other stars of the sky
Became a white mist in the atmosphere,
And by this they knew that the coming was near
   Of the Prince foretold in the prophecy.

Three caskets they bore on their saddle-bows,
   Three caskets of gold with golden keys;
Their robes were of crimson silk with rows
Of bells and pomegranates and furbelows,
   Their turbans like blossoming almond-trees.

And so the Three Kings rode into the West,
  Through the dusk of the night, over hill and dell,
And sometimes they nodded with beard on breast,
And sometimes talked, as they paused to rest,
  With the people they met at some wayside well.

'Of the child that is born,' said Baltasar,
  'Good people, I pray you, tell us the news;
For we in the East have seen his star,
And have ridden fast, and have ridden far,
  To find and worship the King of the Jews.'

And the people answered, 'You ask in vain;
  We know of no king but Herod the Great!'
They thought the Wise Men were men insane,
As they spurred their horses across the plain,
  Like riders in haste, and who cannot wait.

And when they came to Jerusalem,
  Herod the Great, who had heard this thing,
Sent for the Wise Men and questioned them;
And said, 'Go down unto Bethlehem,
  And bring me tidings of this new king.'

So they rode away; and the star stood still,
  The only one in the gray of morn;
Yes, it stopped, it stood still of its own free will,
Right over Bethlehem on the hill,
  The city of David, where Christ was born.

And the Three Kings rode through the gate and
  the guard,
   Through the silent street, till their horses turned
And neighed as they entered the great inn-yard;
But the windows were closed, and the doors were
  barred,
   And only a light in the stable burned.

And cradled there in the scented hay,
   In the air made sweet by the breath of kine,
The little child in the manger lay,
The child, that would be king one day
   Of a kingdom not human but divine.

His mother Mary of Nazareth
   Sat watching beside his place of rest,
Watching the even flow of his breath,
For the joy of life and the terror of death
   Were mingled together in her breast.

They laid their offerings at his feet:
   The gold was their tribute to a King,
The frankincense, with its odor sweet,
Was for the Priest, the Paraclete,
   The myrrh for the body's burying.

And the mother wondered and bowed her head,
   And sat as still as a statue of stone,
Her heart was troubled yet comforted,
Remembering what the Angel had said
   Of an endless reign and of David's throne.

Then the Kings rode out of the city gate,
   With a clatter of hoofs in proud array;
But they went not back to Herod the Great,
For they knew his malice and feared his hate,
   And returned to their homes by another way.

Loss and Gain

Henry Wadsworth Longfellow

A poem of encouragement for those who feel their life has not followed the path they would have liked and want to do better with what life remains to them.

   When I compare
What I have lost with what I have gained,
What I have missed with what attained,
   Little room do I find for pride.

I am aware
How many days have been idly spent;
How like an arrow the good intent
   Has fallen short or been turned aside.

But who shall dare
To measure loss and gain in this wise?
Defeat may be victory in disguise;
   The lowest ebb is the turn of the tide.

To Althea, from Prison

Richard Lovelace (1618–1657)

Richard Lovelace was a Royalist (a supporter of King Charles I). He wrote this poem in 1642 while in prison for presenting a Royalist petition to a Parliament that was at the time hostile to the King.

When Love with unconfinèd wings
   Hovers within my gates,
And my divine Althea brings
   To whisper at the grates;
When I lie tangled in her hair
   And fetter'd to her eye,
The Gods that wanton in the air
   Know no such liberty.

When flowing cups run swiftly round,
  With no allaying Thames,
Our careless heads with roses crown'd,
  Our hearts with loyal flames;
When thirsty grief in wine we steep,
  When healths and draughts go free —
Fishes that tipple in the deep
  Know no such liberty.

When, like committed linnets, I
  With shriller throat shall sing
The sweetness, mercy, majesty,
  And glories of my King;
When I shall voice aloud how good
  He is, how great should be,
Enlargèd winds, that curl the flood,
  Know no such liberty.

Stone walls do not a prison make,
  Nor iron bars a cage;
Minds innocent and quiet take
  That for an hermitage.
If I have freedom in my love,
  And in my soul am free,
Angels alone, that soar above,
  Enjoy such liberty.

To His Coy Mistress

Andrew Marvell (1621–1678)

Andrew Marvell was an English poet, satirist and politician. A man of moderate political opinions, he was a supporter of King Charles I, accepted the republican rule of Oliver Cromwell, and supported the Restoration of the monarchy under Charles II; but the corruption of the court led him eventually to oppose the monarchy. Most of his poetry was not published until after his death.

Had we but World enough, and Time,
This coyness, Lady, were no crime.
We would sit down, and think which way
To walk, and pass our long Love's day.
Thou by the Indian Ganges' side
Should'st Rubies find: I by the tide
Of Humber would complain. I would
Love you ten years before the Flood:
And you should, if you please, refuse
Till the conversion of the Jews.
My vegetable Love should grow
Vaster than Empires, and more slow.

An hundred years should go to praise
Thine Eyes, and on thy Forehead Gaze;
Two hundred to adore each Breast;
But thirty thousand to the rest.
An Age at least to every part,
And the last Age should show your Heart.
For Lady, you deserve this State;
Nor would I love at lower rate.
　But at my back I always hear
Times wingèd Chariot hurrying near:
And yonder all before us lie
Deserts of vast Eternity.
Thy Beauty shall no more be found;
Nor, in thy marble Vault, shall sound
My echoing Song: then Worms shall try
That long preserv'd Virginity:
And your quaint Honour turn to dust;
And into ashes all my Lust.
The Grave's a fine and private place,
But none I think do there embrace.
　Now therefore, while the youthful hue

Sits on thy skin like morning dew,
And while thy willing Soul transpires
At every pore with instant Fires,
Now let us sport us while we may;
And now, like am'rous birds of prey,
Rather at once our Time devour,
Than languish in his slow-chapt pow'r.
Let us roll all our Strength, and all
Our sweetness, up into one Ball:
And tear our Pleasures with rough strife,
Thorough the Iron gates of Life.
Thus, though we cannot make our Sun
Stand still, yet we will make him run.

The Humber is a river estuary in the north of
England on which stands the city of Kingston upon
Hull (often simply known as Hull); Marvell was
Member of Parliament for Hull. 'Slow-chapt power'
pictures Time slowly and inexorably devouring the
potential lovers.

Cargoes

John Masefield (1878–1967)

John Masefield was an English poet and novelist, best known for his poems about the sea. After leaving school, Masefield served an apprenticeship on a sailing ship but ill health forced him to give this up. Nonetheless his love of the sea can be clearly seen in his poetry.

Quinquireme of Nineveh from distant Ophir
Rowing home to haven in sunny Palestine,
With a cargo of ivory,
And apes and peacocks,
Sandalwood, cedarwood, and sweet white wine.

Stately Spanish galleon coming from the Isthmus,
Dipping through the Tropics by the palm-green shores,
With a cargo of diamonds,
Emeralds, amethysts,
Topazes, and cinnamon, and gold moidores.

Dirty British coaster with a salt-caked smoke stack,
Butting through the Channel in the mad March days,
With a cargo of Tyne coal,
Road-rails, pig-lead,
Firewood, iron-ware, and cheap tin trays.

Sea-Fever

John Masefield

I must down to the seas again, to the lonely sea and the sky,
And all I ask is a tall ship and a star to steer her by,
And the wheel's kick and the wind's song and the white
   sails shaking,
And a grey mist on the sea's face, and a grey dawn breaking.

I must down to the seas again, for the call of the running
   tide
Is a wild call and a clear call that may not be denied;
And all I ask is a windy day with the white clouds flying,
And the flung spray and the blown spume, and the sea-
   gulls crying.

I must down to the seas again, to the vagrant gypsy life,
To the gull's way and the whale's way, where the wind's
   like a whetted knife;
And all I ask is a merry yarn from a laughing fellow-rover,
And quiet sleep and a sweet dream when the long trick's
   over.

The first lines of each stanza were originally and are
still sometimes written '... must go down ...' but
Masefield preferred the rhythm of the lines without
the word 'go'.

In Flanders Fields

John McCrae (1872–1918)

In Flanders Fields must be one of the best-known poems from World War I. John McCrae was a Canadian surgeon serving with an artillery brigade of the Canadian Expeditionary Force in Europe. The poem was inspired by the death in 1915 of his friend Lt. Alexis Helmer in the Second Battle of Ypres.

Although less well known, *We Shall Keep the Faith* by Moina Michael (on page 149) is a reply to McCrae's poem.

In Flanders fields the poppies blow
Between the crosses, row on row,
That mark our place; and in the sky
The larks, still bravely singing, fly
Scarce heard amid the guns below.

We are the Dead. Short days ago
We lived, felt dawn, saw sunset glow,
Loved and were loved, and now we lie
  In Flanders fields.

Take up our quarrel with the foe:
To you from failing hands we throw
The torch; be yours to hold it high.
If ye break faith with us who die
We shall not sleep, though poppies grow
 In Flanders fields.

I So Liked Spring

Charlotte Mew (1869–1928)

Charlotte Mew was an English poet and short-story
writer, born in London. Although she is not very
well known now, Thomas Hardy praised her as the
best woman poet of her day.

I so liked Spring last year
 Because you were here; —
 The thrushes too —
Because it was these you so liked to hear —
 I so liked you.

 This year's a different thing, —
 I'll not think of you.
But I'll like the Spring because it is simply Spring
 As the thrushes do.

We Shall Keep the Faith

Moina Michael (1869–1944)

Moina Michael was an American university professor and humanitarian who wrote this poem in response to John McCrae's *In Flanders Fields* (see page 147). She vowed always to wear a red poppy in remembrance, and it was she who had the idea of selling poppies to raise funds for disabled war veterans and their families.

Oh! you who sleep in 'Flanders Fields',
Sleep sweet — to rise anew!
We caught the torch you threw
And holding high, we keep the Faith
  With All who died.

We cherish, too, the poppy red
That grows on fields where valor led;
It seems to signal to the skies
That blood of heroes never dies,
But lends a lustre to the red
Of the flower that blooms above the dead
  In Flanders Fields.

And now the Torch and Poppy Red
We wear in honor of our dead.
Fear not that ye have died for naught;
We'll teach the lesson that ye wrought
  In Flanders Fields.

'Twas the Night Before Christmas

Clement Clarke Moore (1779–1863)

This poem was originally entitled *A Visit from St Nicholas*. There are now many versions differing one from the other in small ways: the names of the last two reindeer were, for example, originally given as 'Dunder' and 'Blixem'.
  Authorship of the poem has also been attributed to Henry Livingston.

'Twas the night before Christmas, when all through the
  house
Not a creature was stirring, not even a mouse;
The stockings were hung by the chimney with care,
In hopes that St Nicholas soon would be there.
The children were nestled all snug in their beds,
While visions of sugar-plums danced in their heads;

And Mamma in her 'kerchief, and I in my cap,
Had just settled our brains for a long winter's nap,
When out on the lawn there arose such a clatter,
I sprang from my bed to see what was the matter.
Away to the window I flew like a flash,
Tore open the shutters and threw up the sash.
The moon on the breast of the new-fallen snow
Gave the lustre of mid-day to objects below.
When what to my wondering eyes should appear,
But a miniature sleigh, and eight tiny reindeer.
With a little old driver, so lively and quick,
I knew in a moment it must be St Nick.
More rapid than eagles his coursers they came,
And he whistled, and shouted, and called them by name:
'Now, Dasher! now, Dancer! now, Prancer and Vixen!
On, Comet! On, Cupid! On, Donder and Blitzen!
To the top of the porch! to the top of the wall!
Now, dash away! dash away! dash away all!'
As dry leaves that before the wild hurricane fly,
When they meet with an obstacle, mount to the sky,
So up to the house-top the coursers they flew,
With the sleigh full of toys – and St Nicholas too.
And then, in a twinkling, I heard on the roof
The prancing and pawing of each little hoof.
As I drew in my head, and was turning around,
Down the chimney St Nicholas came with a bound.
He was dressed all in fur, from his head to his foot,
And his clothes were all tarnished with ashes and soot;
A bundle of toys he had flung on his back,
And he looked like a peddler, just opening his pack.

His eyes – how they twinkled! His dimples, how merry!
His cheeks were like roses, his nose like a cherry!
His droll little mouth was drawn up like a bow,
And the beard of his chin was as white as the snow;
The stump of a pipe he held tight in his teeth,
And the smoke it encircled his head like a wreath.
He had a broad face and a little round belly,
That shook when he laughed, like a bowlful of jelly!
He was chubby and plump, a right jolly old elf,
And I laughed when I saw him, in spite of myself;
A wink of his eye and a twist of his head,
Soon gave me to know I had nothing to dread.
He spoke not a word, but went straight to his work,
And filled all the stockings, then turned with a jerk.
And laying his finger aside of his nose,
And giving a nod, up the chimney he rose;
He sprang to his sleigh, to his team gave a whistle,
And away they all flew like the down of a thistle.
But I heard him exclaim, ere he drove out of sight,
'Happy Christmas to all, and to all a good night!'

This is another poem where visualizing the scene
and the action while reading it over several
times will help to fix the words in your mind. It is
sometimes printed in four-line stanzas, and taking
the poem four lines at a time might well be the best
approach to memorizing it.

The Things That Matter

E Nesbit (1858–1924)

> Edith Nesbit, who published under the name
> E Nesbit, was an English writer perhaps now best
> known for her children's stories such as *The Railway
> Children* and *Five Children and It*.
>   This is a lovely poem that expresses the
> frustration of someone who has lived a long life
> and learnt a great deal, but fears that her fund of
> knowledge will be lost when she is gone.

Now that I've nearly done my days,
  And grown too stiff to sweep or sew,
I sit and think, till I'm amaze,
  About what lots of things I know:
Things as I've found out one by one —
  And when I'm fast down in the clay,
My knowing things and how they're done
  Will all be lost and thrown away.

There's things, I know, as won't be lost,
  Things as folks write and talk about:
The way to keep your roots from frost,
  And how to get your ink spots out.
What medicine's good for sores and sprains,
  What way to salt your butter down,
What charms will cure your different pains,
  And what will bright your faded gown.

But more important things than these,
  They can't be written in a book:
How fast to boil your greens and peas,
  And how good bacon ought to look;
The feel of real good wearing stuff,
  The kind of apple as will keep,
The look of bread that's rose enough,
  And how to get a child asleep.

Whether the jam is fit to pot,
  Whether the milk is going to turn,
Whether a hen will lay or not,
  Is things as some folks never learn.
I know the weather by the sky,
  I know what herbs grow in what lane;
And if sick men are going to die,
  Or if they'll get about again.

Young wives come in, a-smiling, grave,
  With secrets that they itch to tell:
I know what sort of times they'll have,
  And if they'll have a boy or gell.
And if a lad is ill to bind,
  Or some young maid is hard to lead,
I know when you should speak 'em kind,
  And when it's scolding as they need.

I used to know where birds ud set,
  And likely spots for trout or hare,
And God may want me to forget
  The way to set a line or snare;
But not the way to truss a chick,
  To fry a fish, or baste a roast,
Nor how to tell, when folks are sick,
  What kind of herb will ease them most!

Forgetting seems such silly waste!
  I know so many little things,
And now the Angels will make haste
  To dust it all away with wings!
O God, you made me like to know,
  You kept the things straight in my head,
Please God, if you can make it so,
  Let me know *something* when I'm dead.

'*Gell*' represents a particular English pronunciation of *girl*; '*ud*' = would.

Annabel Lee

Edgar Allan Poe (1809–1849)

Edgar Allan Poe was an American poet, story writer and journalist. Much of his prose and poetry deals with the macabre and mysterious; in some of his tales, Poe could be considered a pioneer of the modern detective story.

It was many and many a year ago,
  In a kingdom by the sea,
That a maiden there lived whom you may know
  By the name of Annabel Lee;
And this maiden she lived with no other thought
  Than to love and be loved by me.

I was a child and she was a child,
  In this kingdom by the sea,
But we loved with a love that was more than love —
  I and my Annabel Lee —
With a love that the wingèd seraphs of heaven
  Coveted her and me.

And this was the reason that, long ago,
  In this kingdom by the sea,
A wind blew out of a cloud, chilling
  My beautiful Annabel Lee;
So that her highborn kinsmen came
  And bore her away from me,
To shut her up in a sepulchre
  In this kingdom by the sea.

The angels, not half so happy in heaven,
  Went envying her and me —
 Yes! – that was the reason (as all men know,
  In this kingdom by the sea)
That the wind came out of the cloud by night,
  Chilling and killing my Annabel Lee.

But our love it was stronger by far than the love
  Of those who were older than we —
  Of many far wiser than we —
And neither the angels in heaven above,
  Nor the demons down under the sea,
Can ever dissever my soul from the soul
  Of the beautiful Annabel Lee.

For the moon never beams without bringing me dreams
  Of the beautiful Annabel Lee;
And the stars never rise but I feel the bright eyes
  Of the beautiful Annabel Lee;
And so, all the night-tide, I lie down by the side
Of my darling — my darling — my life and my bride,
  In her sepulchre there by the sea —
  In her tomb by the sounding sea.

> Notice that the verses in this poem have different
> numbers of lines, and the rhyme scheme is
> therefore not quite the same in every verse.

Eldorado

Edgar Allan Poe

  Gaily bedight,
  A gallant knight,
In sunshine and in shadow,
  Had journeyed long,
  Singing a song,
In search of Eldorado.

Edgar Allan Poe

But he grew old —
  This knight so bold —
And o'er his heart a shadow
  Fell as he found
  No spot of ground
That looked like Eldorado.

And, as his strength
  Failed him at length,
He met a pilgrim shadow —
  'Shadow,' said he,
  'Where can it be —
This land of Eldorado?'

'Over the Mountains
  Of the Moon,
Down the Valley of the Shadow,
  Ride, boldly ride,'
  The shade replied —
'If you seek for Eldorado!'

159

The Raven

Edgar Allan Poe

Once upon a midnight dreary, while I pondered,
  weak and weary,
Over many a quaint and curious volume of
  forgotten lore —
While I nodded, nearly napping, suddenly there
  came a tapping,
As of some one gently rapping, rapping at my
  chamber door.
' 'Tis some visitor,' I muttered, 'tapping at my
  chamber door —
Only this, and nothing more.'

Ah, distinctly I remember it was in the bleak
  December;
And each separate dying ember wrought its ghost
  upon the floor.
Eagerly I wished the morrow; — vainly I had
  sought to borrow
From my books surcease of sorrow — sorrow for
  the lost Lenore —
For the rare and radiant maiden whom the angels
  name Lenore —
Nameless *here* for evermore.

And the silken, sad, uncertain rustling of each
   purple curtain
Thrilled me — filled me with fantastic terrors
   never felt before;
So that now, to still the beating of my heart, I
   stood repeating
' 'Tis some visitor entreating entrance at my
   chamber door —
Some late visitor entreating entrance at my
   chamber door; —
This it is and nothing more.'

Presently my soul grew stronger; hesitating then
   no longer,
'Sir,' said I, 'or Madam, truly your forgiveness I
   implore;
But the fact is I was napping, and so gently you
   came rapping,
And so faintly you came tapping, tapping at my
   chamber door,
That I scarce was sure I heard you' — here I
   opened wide the door; —
Darkness there, and nothing more.

Deep into that darkness peering, long I stood
   there wondering, fearing,
Doubting, dreaming dreams no mortal ever dared
   to dream before;
But the silence was unbroken, and the stillness
   gave no token,

And the only word there spoken was the
    whispered word, 'Lenore!'
This I whispered, and an echo murmured back the
    word, 'Lenore!'
Merely this and nothing more.

Back into the chamber turning, all my soul within
    me burning,
Soon again I heard a tapping somewhat louder
    than before.
'Surely,' said I, 'surely that is something at my
    window lattice;
Let me see, then, what thereat is, and this mystery
    explore —
Let my heart be still a moment and this mystery
    explore —
'Tis the wind and nothing more!'

Open here I flung the shutter, when, with many a
    flirt and flutter,
In there stepped a stately Raven of the saintly
    days of yore.
Not the least obeisance made he; not a minute
    stopped or stayed he;
But, with mien of lord or lady, perched above my
    chamber door —
Perched upon a bust of Pallas just above my
    chamber door —
Perched, and sat, and nothing more.

Then this ebony bird beguiling my sad fancy into
  smiling,
By the grave and stern decorum of the
  countenance it wore,
'Though thy crest be shorn and shaven, thou,' I
  said, 'art sure no craven,
Ghastly grim and ancient Raven wandering from
  the Nightly shore —
Tell me what thy lordly name is on the Night's
  Plutonian shore!'
Quoth the Raven, 'Nevermore.'

Much I marvelled this ungainly fowl to hear
  discourse so plainly,
Though its answer little meaning — little
  relevancy bore;
For we cannot help agreeing that no living human
  being
Ever yet was blessed with seeing bird above his
  chamber door —
Bird or beast upon the sculptured bust above his
  chamber door,
With such name as 'Nevermore.'

But the Raven, sitting lonely on the placid bust,
  spoke only
That one word, as if his soul in that one word he
  did outpour.
Nothing further then he uttered — not a feather
  then he fluttered —

Till I scarcely more than muttered 'Other friends
  have flown before —
On the morrow *he* will leave me, as my hopes
  have flown before.'
Then the bird said, 'Nevermore.'

Startled at the stillness broken by reply so aptly
  spoken,
'Doubtless,' said I, 'what it utters is its only stock
  and store
Caught from some unhappy master whom
  unmerciful Disaster
Followed fast and followed faster till his songs one
  burden bore —
Till the dirges of his Hope that melancholy
  burden bore
Of "Never — nevermore".'

But the Raven still beguiling my sad fancy into
  smiling,
Straight I wheeled a cushioned seat in front of
  bird and bust and door;
Then, upon the velvet sinking, I betook myself to
  linking
Fancy unto fancy, thinking what this ominous bird
  of yore —
What this grim, ungainly, ghastly, gaunt, and
  ominous bird of yore
Meant in croaking 'Nevermore.'

This I sat engaged in guessing, but no syllable
  expressing
To the fowl whose fiery eyes now burned into my
  bosom's core;
This and more I sat divining, with my head at ease
  reclining
On the cushion's velvet lining that the lamp-light
  gloated o'er,
But whose velvet violet lining with the lamp-light
  gloating o'er,
She shall press, ah, nevermore!

Then, methought, the air grew denser, perfumed
  from an unseen censer
Swung by seraphim whose foot-falls tinkled on
  the tufted floor.
'Wretch,' I cried, 'thy God hath lent thee — by
  these angels he has sent thee
Respite — respite and nepenthe from thy
  memories of Lenore!
Quaff, oh quaff this kind nepenthe, and forget this
  lost Lenore!'
Quoth the raven, 'Nevermore.'

'Prophet!' said I, 'thing of evil! — prophet still, if
  bird or devil! —
Whether Tempter sent, or whether tempest tossed
  thee here ashore,
Desolate yet all undaunted, on this desert land
  enchanted —

On this home by Horror haunted — tell me truly,
    I implore —
Is there — *is* there balm in Gilead? — tell me —
    tell me, I implore!'
Quoth the Raven, 'Nevermore.'

'Prophet!' said I, 'thing of evil! — prophet still, if
    bird or devil!
By that Heaven that bends above us — by that
    God we both adore —
Tell this soul with sorrow laden if, within the
    distant Aidenn,
It shall clasp a sainted maiden whom the angels
    name Lenore —
Clasp a rare and radiant maiden, whom the angels
    name Lenore.'
Quoth the Raven, 'Nevermore.'

'Be that word our sign of parting, bird or fiend!' I
    shrieked, upstarting —
'Get thee back into the tempest and the Night's
    Plutonian shore!
Leave no black plume as a token of that lie thy
    soul hath spoken!
Leave my loneliness unbroken! — quit the bust
    above my door!
Take thy beak from out my heart, and take thy
    form from off my door!'
Quoth the Raven, 'Nevermore.'

And the Raven, never flitting, still is sitting, *still* is
    sitting
On the pallid bust of Pallas just above my
    chamber door;
And his eyes have all the seeming of a demon's
    that is dreaming,
And the lamp-light o'er him streaming throws his
    shadow on the floor;
And my soul from out that shadow that lies
    floating on the floor
Shall be lifted — nevermore!

This is a long poem to learn – though some readers may relish the challenge! – but the rhythm, internal rhymes and repetitions draw you on from verse to verse, which makes it easier to memorize. If the poem appeals to you but you find the length daunting, you could easily omit sections that are less important to the development of the story (for example stanzas 4, 5 and 6), which would make memorization more manageable.

Pallas is the Greek goddess Pallas Athene, the goddess of wisdom; 'Aidenn' is a poetic spelling of Eden, i.e. paradise; nepenthe is a drug that brings forgetfulness of grief; 'balm in Gilead' is a reference to Jeremiah 8:22 in the Bible.

The girl *Lenore* is also the subject of Poe's poem 'Lenore'.

An Essay on Man: Epistle 2

Alexander Pope (1688–1744)

Alexander Pope was an English poet and satirist. This extract from his long poem, *An Essay on Man*, is a reflection on religion, humanity and reason.

Know then thyself, presume not God to scan;
The proper study of mankind is Man.
Placed on this isthmus of a middle state,
A being darkly wise, and rudely great:
With too much knowledge for the Sceptic side,
With too much weakness for the Stoic's pride,
He hangs between; in doubt to act or rest;
In doubt to deem himself a God or Beast;
In doubt his mind or body to prefer;
Born but to die, and reasoning but to err;
Alike in ignorance, his reason such
Whether he thinks too little or too much:
Chaos of thought and passion, all confused;
Still by himself abused, or disabused;
Created half to rise and half to fall;
Great lord of all things, yet a prey to all;
Sole judge of truth, in endless error hurled:
The glory, jest, and riddle of the world!

Naming of Parts

Henry Reed (1914–1986)

I have liked this poem since a friend of mine recited it to me. In it, Reed contrasts the weapons of war with the beauties of nature. It is the first and best-known poem in a series called *Lessons of the War.*

To-day we have naming of parts. Yesterday,
We had daily cleaning. And to-morrow morning,
We shall have what to do after firing. But to-day,
To-day we have naming of parts. Japonica
Glistens like coral in all the neighbouring gardens,
    And to-day we have naming of parts.

This is the lower sling swivel. And this
Is the upper sling swivel, whose use you will see,
When you are given your slings. And this is the piling
    swivel,
Which in your case you have not got. The branches
Hold in the gardens their silent, eloquent gestures,
    Which in our case we have not got.

This is the safety-catch, which is always released
With an easy flick of the thumb. And please do not let
    me

See anyone using his finger. You can do it quite easy
If you have any strength in your thumb. The blossoms
Are fragile and motionless, never letting anyone see
    Any of them using their finger.

And this you can see is the bolt. The purpose of this
Is to open the breech, as you see. We can slide it
Rapidly backwards and forwards: we call this
Easing the spring. And rapidly backwards and forwards
The early bees are assaulting and fumbling the flowers:
    They call it easing the Spring.

They call it easing the Spring: it is perfectly easy
If you have any strength in your thumb: like the bolt,
And the breech, the cocking-piece, and the point of
    balance,
Which in our case we have not got; and the almond
    blossom
Silent in all of the gardens and the bees going backwards
    and forwards,
    For to-day we have naming of parts.

There are two people speaking in this poem:
the British army rifle instructor and the recruit
witnessing the demonstration. When learning (and
reciting) this poem, try to distinguish between the
two voices.

Remember

Christina Rossetti (1830–1894)

Christina Rossetti was the sister of the artist and poet Dante Gabriel Rossetti. Much of her poetry is on religious themes. She wrote the words to the famous Christmas carol 'In the Bleak Mid-Winter'.

Remember me when I am gone away,
  Gone far away into the silent land;
  When you can no more hold me by the hand,
Nor I half turn to go yet turning stay.
Remember me when no more day by day
  You tell me of our future that you planned:
  Only remember me; you understand
It will be late to counsel then or pray.
Yet if you should forget me for a while
  And afterwards remember, do not grieve:
  For if the darkness and corruption leave
A vestige of the thoughts that once I had,
Better by far you should forget and smile
  Than that you should remember and be sad.

Song

Christina Rossetti

When I am dead, my dearest,
  Sing no sad songs for me;
Plant thou no roses at my head,
  Nor shady cypress tree:
Be the green grass above me
  With showers and dewdrops wet;
And if thou wilt, remember,
  And if thou wilt, forget.

I shall not see the shadows,
  I shall not feel the rain;
I shall not hear the nightingale
  Sing on, as if in pain;
And dreaming through the twilight
  That doth not rise nor set,
Haply I may remember,
  And haply may forget.

Uphill

Christina Rossetti

Does the road wind uphill all the way?
  Yes, to the very end.
Will the day's journey take the whole long day?
  From morn to night, my friend.

But is there for the night a resting-place?
  A roof for when the slow, dark hours begin.
May not the darkness hide it from my face?
  You cannot miss that inn.

Shall I meet other wayfarers at night?
  Those who have gone before.
Then must I knock, or call when just in sight?
  They will not keep you waiting at that door.

Shall I find comfort, travel-sore and weak?
  Of labour you shall find the sum.
Will there be beds for me and all who seek?
  Yea, beds for all who come.

Sudden Light

Dante Gabriel Rossetti (1828–1882)

Dante Gabriel Rossetti was the brother of Christina Rossetti. He was a poet, artist and leading member of the Pre-Raphaelite Brotherhood. In 1862, grief drove him to bury the only complete manuscript of his poetry with the coffin of his late wife Elizabeth, but the poems were exhumed in 1869 and published the following year.

I have been here before,
    But when or how I cannot tell:
I know the grass beyond the door,
    The sweet keen smell,
The sighing sound, the lights around the shore.

    You have been mine before, —
        How long ago I may not know:
    But just when at that swallow's soar
        Your neck turned so,
    Some veil did fall, — I knew it all of yore.

    Has this been thus before?
        And shall not thus time's eddying flight
    Still with our lives our love restore
        In death's despite,
    And day and night yield one delight once more?

The River

Frederick George Scott (1861–1944)

> Frederick George Scott was a Canadian poet and
> writer and an Anglican priest. Often called 'The
> Poet of the Laurentians', he produced 13 volumes
> of poetry, much of it strongly patriotic (he was
> a strong supporter of the British Empire) or on
> Christian themes.

Why hurry, little river,
   Why hurry to the sea?
There is nothing there to do
But to sink into the blue
   And all forgotten be.
There is nothing on that shore
But the tides for evermore,
And the faint and far-off line
Where the winds across the brine
For ever, ever roam
And never find a home.

Why hurry, little river,
    From the mountains and the mead,
Where the graceful elms are sleeping
    And the quiet cattle feed?
The loving shadows cool
The deep and restful pool,
And every tribute stream
Brings its own sweet woodland dream
Of the mighty woods that sleep
Where the sighs of earth are deep,
And the silent skies look down
On the savage mountain's frown.

Oh, linger, little river,
    Your banks are all so fair,
Each morning is a hymn of praise,
    Each evening is a prayer.
All day the sunbeams glitter
    On your shallows and your bars,
And at night the dear God stills you
    With the music of the stars.

The Unnamed Lake

Frederick George Scott

Scott wrote this poem at St Raymond in Quebec.
While out with his children, he came to the top of
a hill and saw a lake lying in front of them between
the mountains.

It sleeps among the thousand hills
　　Where no man ever trod,
And only nature's music fills
　　The silences of God.

Great mountains tower above its shore,
　　Green rushes fringe its brim,
And o'er its breast for evermore
　　The wanton breezes skim.

Dark clouds that intercept the sun
　　Go there in Spring to weep,
And there, when Autumn days are done,
　　White mists lie down to sleep.

Sunrise and sunset crown with gold
   The peaks of ageless stone,
Where winds have thundered from of old
   And storms have set their throne.

No echoes of the world afar
   Disturb it night or day,
But sun and shadow, moon and star,
   Pass and repass for aye.

'Twas in the grey of early dawn,
   When first the lake we spied,
And fragments of a cloud were drawn
   Half down the mountain side.

Along the shore a heron flew,
   And from a speck on high,
That hovered in the deepening blue,
   We heard the fish-hawk's cry.

Among the cloud-capt solitudes,
   No sound the silence broke,
Save when, in whispers down the woods,
   The guardian mountains spoke.

Through tangled brush and dewy brake,
   Returning whence we came,
We passed in silence, and the lake
   We left without a name.

The Call of the Wild

Robert Service (1874–1958)

Robert Service was born in England, but emigrated to Canada at the age of 21. While employed as a banker, he spent some years in the Yukon which forms the scene of some of his popular poetic tales, such as 'The Shooting of Dan McGrew'. He has been called 'The Bard of the Yukon' and 'The Canadian Kipling'. Much of Service's poetry is very rhythmic and song-like, which makes it easier to learn. In this poem you can feel the rhythm pulling you on from line to line.

Have you gazed on naked grandeur, where there's
   nothing else to gaze on,
Set pieces and drop-curtain scenes galore,
Big mountains heaved to heaven, which the
   blinding sunsets blazon,
Black canyons where the rapids rip and roar?
Have you swept the visioned valley with the green
   stream streaking through it,
Searched the Vastness for a something you have
   lost?
Have you strung your soul to silence? Then for
   God's sake go and do it;
Hear the challenge, learn the lesson, pay the cost.

Have you wandered in the wilderness, the
    sagebrush desolation,
The bunch-grass levels where the cattle graze?
Have you whistled bits of rag-time at the end of
    all creation,
And learned to know the desert's little ways?
Have you camped upon the foothills, have you
    galloped o'er the ranges,
Have you roamed the arid sun-lands through and
    through?
Have you chummed up with the mesa? Do you
    know its moods and changes?
Then listen to the Wild – it's calling you.

Have you known the Great White Silence, not a
    snow-gemmed twig aquiver?
(Eternal truths that shame our soothing lies.)
Have you broken trail on snowshoes? mushed
    your Huskies up the river,
Dared the unknown, led the way, and clutched
    the prize?
Have you marked the map's void spaces, mingled
    with the mongrel races,
Felt the savage strength of brute in every thew?
And though grim as hell the worst is, can you
    round it off with curses?
Then hearken to the Wild – it's wanting you.

Have you suffered, starved, and triumphed,
    grovelled down, yet grasped at glory,

Grown bigger in the bigness of the whole?
'Done things' just for the doing, letting babblers
    tell the story,
Seeing through the nice veneer the naked soul?
Have you seen God in His splendours, heard the
    text that nature renders?
(You'll never hear it in the family pew),
The simple things, the true things, the silent men
    who do things?
Then listen to the Wild – it's calling you.

They have cradled you in custom, they have
    primed you with their preaching,
They have soaked you in convention through and
    through;
They have put you in a showcase; you're a credit
    to their teaching –
But can't you hear the wild? – it's calling you.
Let us probe the silent places, let us seek what
    luck betide us;
Let us journey to a lonely land I know.
There's a whisper on the night-wind, there's a star
    agleam to guide us,
And the Wild is calling, calling . . . let us go.

Each Day a Life

Robert Service

I count each day a little life,
With birth and death complete;
I cloister it from care and strife
And keep it sane and sweet.

With eager eyes I greet the morn,
Exultant as a boy,
Knowing that I am newly born
To wonder and to joy.

And when the sunset splendours wane
And ripe for rest am I,
Knowing that I will live again,
Exultantly I die.

O that all Life were but a Day
Sunny and sweet and sane!
And that at Even I might say:
'I sleep to wake again.'

Sonnet 18

Shall I Compare Thee to a Summer's Day?

William Shakespeare (1564–1616)

Shakespeare must be the most quoted poet and dramatist of all time, yet for many of us our only acquaintance with him is during our schooldays, when we may not be ready to appreciate him fully. Among his purely poetical works, Shakespeare wrote a series of 154 sonnets. Three of the best-loved of these sonnets are included here.

Shall I compare thee to a summer's day?
Thou art more lovely and more temperate.
Rough winds do shake the darling buds of May,
And summer's lease hath all too short a date:
Sometime too hot the eye of heaven shines,
And often is his gold complexion dimm'd;
And every fair from fair sometime declines,
By chance, or nature's changing course, untrimm'd;
But thy eternal summer shall not fade,
Nor lose possession of that fair thou ow'st;
Nor shall Death brag thou wand'rest in his shade,
When in eternal lines to time thou grow'st.
    So long as men can breathe or eyes can see,
    So long lives this, and this gives life to thee.

Sonnet 116

Let Me Not to the Marriage of True Minds

William Shakespeare

Let me not to the marriage of true minds
Admit impediments. Love is not love
Which alters when it alteration finds,
Or bends with the remover to remove:
O, no! It is an ever-fixèd mark
That looks on tempests and is never shaken;
It is the star to every wand'ring bark,
Whose worth's unknown, although his height be taken.
Love's not Time's fool, though rosy lips and cheeks
Within his bending sickle's compass come;
Love alters not with his brief hours and weeks,
But bears it out even to the edge of doom.
   If this be error and upon me prov'd,
    I never writ, nor no man ever lov'd.

Sonnet 130

My Mistress' Eyes Are Nothing Like the Sun

William Shakespeare

My mistress' eyes are nothing like the sun;
Coral is far more red than her lips' red;
If snow be white, why then her breasts are dun;
If hairs be wires, black wires grow on her head.
I have seen roses damask'd, red and white,
But no such roses see I in her cheeks;
And in some perfumes is there more delight
Than in the breath that from my mistress reeks.
I love to hear her speak, yet well I know
That music hath a far more pleasing sound;
I grant I never saw a goddess go –
My mistress when she walks treads on the ground.
  And yet, by heaven, I think my love as rare
  As any she belied with false compare.

But, Soft! What Light Through Yonder Window Breaks?

William Shakespeare

> The verses on the next three pages are from *Romeo and Juliet*. The first speech is made by Romeo when he sees Juliet on her balcony.

But, soft! What light through yonder window
   breaks?
It is the east, and Juliet is the sun.
Arise, fair sun, and kill the envious moon,
Who is already sick and pale with grief
That thou, her maid, art far more fair than she.
Be not her maid, since she is envious;
Her vestal livery is but sick and green,
And none but fools do wear it; cast it off.

It is my lady; O, it is my love!
O that she knew she were!
She speaks, yet she says nothing. What of that?
Her eye discourses; I will answer it.
I am too bold, 'tis not to me she speaks;
Two of the fairest stars in all the heaven,
Having some business, do entreat her eyes
To twinkle in their spheres till they return.
What if her eyes were there, they in her head?
The brightness of her cheek would shame those
    stars,
As daylight doth a lamp; her eyes in heaven
Would through the airy region stream so bright
That birds would sing and think it were not night.
See how she leans her cheek upon her hand!
O that I were a glove upon that hand,
That I might touch that cheek!

O Romeo, Romeo! Wherefore Art Thou Romeo?

William Shakespeare

O Romeo, Romeo! Wherefore art thou Romeo?
Deny thy father and refuse thy name;
Or, if thou wilt not, be but sworn my love,
And I'll no longer be a Capulet.
'Tis but thy name that is my enemy;
Thou art thyself, though not a Montague.
What's Montague? It is nor hand, nor foot,
Nor arm, nor face, nor any other part
Belonging to a man. O, be some other name!
What's in a name? That which we call a rose
By any other name would smell as sweet;
So Romeo would, were he not Romeo called,
Retain that dear perfection which he owes
Without that title. Romeo, doff thy name;
And for that name, which is no part of thee,
Take all myself.

Remember that 'wherefore?' means 'why?', not 'where?'. Many people misunderstand this line, and put the stress on 'art' rather than on 'wherefore'.

If Music Be the Food of Love

William Shakespeare

This is the opening speech of *Twelfth Night*, spoken by Count Orsino.

If music be the food of love, play on,
Give me excess of it, that, surfeiting,
The appetite may sicken, and so die.
That strain again! It had a dying fall:
O, it came o'er my ear like the sweet sound,
That breathes upon a bank of violets,
Stealing and giving odour! Enough; no more;
'Tis not so sweet now as it was before.
O spirit of love! how quick and fresh art thou,
That, notwithstanding thy capacity
Receiveth as the sea, nought enters there,
Of what validity and pitch soe'er,
But falls into abatement and low price,
Even in a minute. So full of shapes is fancy,
That it alone is high fantastical.

To Be, or Not To Be

William Shakespeare

 This famous speech is from Act III of *Hamlet*.

To be, or not to be: that is the question;
Whether 'tis nobler in the mind to suffer
The slings and arrows of outrageous fortune,
Or to take arms against a sea of troubles,
And by opposing end them. To die, to sleep –
No more; and, by a sleep to say we end
The heart-ache and the thousand natural shocks
That flesh is heir to. 'Tis a consummation
Devoutly to be wish'd. To die, to sleep;
To sleep, perchance to dream: ay, there's the rub;
For in that sleep of death what dreams may come
When we have shuffled off this mortal coil,
Must give us pause. There's the respect
That makes calamity of so long life;
For who would bear the whips and scorns of time,
The oppressor's wrong, the proud man's contumely,
The pangs of despis'd love, the law's delay,
The insolence of office, and the spurns

That patient merit of the unworthy takes,
When he himself might his quietus make
With a bare bodkin? Who would fardels bear,
To grunt and sweat under a weary life,
But that the dread of something after death,
The undiscover'd country, from whose bourn
No traveller returns, puzzles the will,
And makes us rather bear those ills we have
Than fly to others that we know not of?
Thus conscience does make cowards of us all;
And thus the native hue of resolution
Is sicklied o'er with the pale cast of thought,
And enterprises of great pitch and moment
With this regard their currents turn awry
And lose the name of action.

'Fardels' in line 21 means 'burdens'.

Tomorrow, and Tomorrow, and Tomorrow

William Shakespeare

> Macbeth's well-known soliloquy on life and death, from Act V of the play.

Tomorrow, and tomorrow, and tomorrow,
Creeps in this petty pace from day to day
To the last syllable of recorded time,
And all our yesterdays have lighted fools
The way to dusty death. Out, out, brief candle!
Life's but a walking shadow, a poor player
That struts and frets his hour upon the stage
And then is heard no more; it is a tale
Told by an idiot, full of sound and fury,
Signifying nothing.

Ozymandias

Percy Bysshe Shelley (1792–1822)

> Ozymandias was the Greek name for Ramses II, one of the greatest of the Egyptian pharaohs. On the base of one statue of Ramses there is an inscription which has been translated into English as 'King of Kings am I, Osymandias. If anyone would know how great I am and where I lie, let him surpass one of my works.' But as Keats says in this poem, 'Look around. There's nothing left of Ozymandias and his works but a broken statue and a lot of sand.' So much for hubris.

I met a traveller from an antique land
Who said: Two vast and trunkless legs of stone
Stand in the desert . . . Near them, on the sand,
Half sunk, a shattered visage lies, whose frown,
And wrinkled lip, and sneer of cold command,
Tell that its sculptor well those passions read
Which yet survive, stamped on these lifeless things,
The hand that mocked them, and the heart that fed:
And on the pedestal these words appear:
'My name is Ozymandias, King of Kings:
Look on my works, ye Mighty, and despair!'
Nothing beside remains. Round the decay
Of that colossal wreck, boundless and bare
The lone and level sands stretch far away.

To a Skylark

Percy Bysshe Shelley

This beautiful poem allows us to share the poet's joy at seeing and listening to the 'profuse strains' of the skylark's song. It is quite long, but too good to be omitted from this collection. If you feel it is too long to memorize, just pick out some of the key stanzas and learn those.

Hail to thee, blithe Spirit!
  Bird thou never wert,
That from Heaven, or near it,
  Pourest thy full heart
In profuse strains of unpremeditated art.

Higher still and higher
  From the earth thou springest
Like a cloud of fire;
  The blue deep thou wingest,
And singing still dost soar, and soaring ever singest.

In the golden light'ning
  Of the sunken sun,
O'er which clouds are bright'ning,
  Thou dost float and run;
Like an unbodied joy whose race is just begun.

The pale purple even
  Melts around thy flight;
Like a star of Heaven,
  In the broad daylight
Thou art unseen, but yet I hear thy shrill delight,

Keen as are the arrows
  Of that silver sphere,
Whose intense lamp narrows
  In the white dawn clear
Until we hardly see – we feel that it is there.

All the earth and air
  With thy voice is loud,
As, when night is bare,
  From one lonely cloud
The moon rains out her beams, and heaven is
  overflowed.

What thou art we know not;
  What is most like thee?
From rainbow clouds there flow not
  Drops so bright to see
As from thy presence showers a rain of melody.

Like a Poet hidden
  In the light of thought,
Singing hymns unbidden,
  Till the world is wrought
To sympathy with hopes and fears it heeded not:

Like a high-born maiden
  In a palace-tower,
Soothing her love-laden
  Soul in secret hour
With music sweet as love, which overflows her
    bower:

Like a glow-worm golden
  In a dell of dew,
Scattering unbeholden
  Its aëreal hue
Among the flowers and grass, which screen it from
    the view!

Like a rose embowered
  In its own green leaves,
By warm winds deflowered,
  Till the scent it gives
Makes faint with too much sweet those heavy-
    wingèd thieves.

Sound of vernal showers
  On the twinkling grass,
Rain-awakened flowers,
  All that ever was
Joyous and clear, and fresh, thy music doth
    surpass:

Teach us, Sprite or Bird,
  What sweet thoughts are thine:
I have never heard
  Praise of love or wine
That panted forth a flood of rapture so divine.

Chorus Hymeneal,
  Or triumphal chant,
Matched with thine would be all
  But an empty vaunt,
A thing wherein we feel there is some hidden
  want.

What objects are the fountains
  Of thy happy strain?
What fields, or waves, or mountains?
  What shapes of sky or plain?
What love of thine own kind? what ignorance of
  pain?

With thy clear keen joyance
  Languor cannot be:
Shadow of annoyance
  Never came near thee:
Thou lovest – but ne'er knew love's sad satiety.

Waking or asleep,
  Thou of death must deem
Things more true and deep

Than we mortals dream,
Or how could thy notes flow in such a crystal
stream?

We look before and after,
  And pine for what is not:
Our sincerest laughter
  With some pain is fraught;
Our sweetest songs are those that tell of saddest
  thought.

Yet, if we could scorn
  Hate, and pride, and fear,
If we were things born
  Not to shed a tear,
I know not how thy joy we ever should come near.

Better than all measures
  Of delightful sound,
Better than all treasures
  That in books are found,
Thy skill to poet were, thou scorner of the ground!

Teach me half the gladness
  That thy brain must know,
Such harmonious madness
  From my lips would flow
The world should listen then – as I am listening
  now.

The Bargain

Sir Philip Sidney (1554–1586)

Sir Philip Sidney was an Elizabethan statesman, poet and patron of the arts. As a writer of sonnets, he is considered second only to Shakespeare, though none of his poetry was published in his lifetime. This sonnet, written as though said by a woman, comes from his romance, *Arcadia*.

My true love hath my heart, and I have his,
　By just exchange one for the other given.
I hold his dear, and mine he cannot miss,
　There never was a bargain better driven.
His heart in me keeps me and him in one,
　My heart in him his thoughts and senses guides;
He loves my heart for once it was his own,
　I cherish his because in me it bides.
His heart his wound receivèd from my sight,
　My heart was wounded with his wounded heart;
For as from me on him his hurt did light,
　So still methought in me his hurt did smart.
　　Both equal hurt, in this change sought our bliss:
　　My true love hath my heart and I have his.

From a Railway Carriage

Robert Louis Stevenson (1850–1894)

Robert Louis Stevenson was a Scottish author and poet. Among his novels are *Treasure Island*, *Kidnapped* and *The Strange Case of Dr Jekyll and Mr Hyde*. Among his poetical works are *A Child's Garden of Verses*.

As you read these lines, feel the rhythm of the train as it thunders along. I often wish that Stevenson had written more than two stanzas for this poem – I feel disappointed when I reach 'gone forever' and the poem stops. It seems too short a journey!

Faster than fairies, faster than witches,
Bridges and houses, hedges and ditches;
And charging along like troops in a battle
All through the meadows the horses and cattle:
All of the sights of the hill and the plain
Fly as thick as driving rain;
And ever again, in the wink of an eye,
Painted stations whistle by.

Here is a child who clambers and scrambles,
All by himself and gathering brambles;
Here is a tramp who stands and gazes;

And there is the green for stringing the daisies!
Here is a cart run away in the road
Lumping along with man and load;
And here is a mill, and there is a river:
Each a glimpse and gone for ever!

I Will Make You Brooches

Robert Louis Stevenson

I will make you brooches and toys for your delight
Of bird-song at morning and star-shine at night.
I will make a palace fit for you and me
Of green days in forests and blue days at sea.

I will make my kitchen, and you shall keep your room,
Where white flows the river and bright blows the broom,
And you shall wash your linen and keep your body white
In rainfall at morning and dewfall at night.

And this shall be for music when no one else is near,
The fine song for singing, the rare song to hear!
That only I remember, that only you admire,
Of the broad road that stretches and the roadside fire.

Small Is the Trust When Love Is Green

Robert Louis Stevenson

Small is the trust when love is green
In sap of early years;
A little thing steps in between
And kisses turn to tears.

A while – and see how love be grown
In loveliness and power!
A while, it loves the sweets alone,
But next it loves the sour.

A little love is none at all
That wanders or that fears;
A hearty love dwells still at call
To kisses or to tears.

Such then be mine, my love, to give,
And such be yours to take: –
A faith to hold, a life to live,
For loving kindness' sake: –

Should you be sad, should you be gay,
  Or should you prove unkind,
A love to hold the growing way
  And keep the helping mind: –

A love to turn the laugh on care
  When wrinkled care appears,
And, with an equal will, to share
  Your losses and your tears.

The White Canoe

Alan Sullivan (1868–1947)

Alan Sullivan was a Canadian engineer, poet and author. A 'white canoe' features in Native American folklore relating to Niagara Falls.

There's a whisper of life in the grey dead trees,
  And a murmuring wash on the shore,
And a breath of the South in the loitering breeze,
  To tell that a winter is o'er.
While free, at last, from its fetters of ice
  The river is clear and blue,
And cries with a tremulous quivering voice
  For the launch of the White Canoe.

Oh, gently the ripples will kiss her side,
   And tenderly bear her on;
For she is the wandering phantom bride
   Of the river she rests upon;
She is loved with a love that cannot forget,
   A passion so strong and true,
That never a billow has risen yet
   To peril the White Canoe.

So come when the moon is enthroned in the sky,
   And the echoes are sweet and low,
And Nature is full of the mystery
   That none but her children know;
Come, taste of the rest that the weary crave,
   But is only revealed to a few:
When there's trouble on shore, there's peace on
   the wave,
   Afloat in the White Canoe.

The Brook

Alfred, Lord Tennyson (1809–1892)

Alfred Tennyson became Poet Laureate in 1850 and
was created a baron (hence 'Lord Tennyson')
in 1884.

I come from haunts of coot and hern,
I make a sudden sally
And sparkle out among the fern,
To bicker down a valley.

By thirty hills I hurry down,
Or slip between the ridges,
By twenty thorps, a little town,
And half a hundred bridges.

Till last by Philip's farm I flow
To join the brimming river,
For men may come and men may go,
But I go on for ever.

I chatter over stony ways,
In little sharps and trebles,
I bubble into eddying bays,
I babble on the pebbles.

With many a curve my banks I fret
By many a field and fallow,
And many a fairy foreland set
With willow-weed and mallow.

I chatter, chatter, as I flow
To join the brimming river,
For men may come and men may go,
But I go on for ever.

I wind about, and in and out,
With here a blossom sailing,
And here and there a lusty trout,
And here and there a grayling,

And here and there a foamy flake
Upon me, as I travel
With many a silver waterbreak
Above the golden gravel,

And draw them all along, and flow
To join the brimming river,
For men may come and men may go,
But I go on for ever.

I steal by lawns and grassy plots,
I slide by hazel covers;
I move the sweet forget-me-nots
That grow for happy lovers.

I slip, I slide, I gloom, I glance,
Among my skimming swallows;
I make the netted sunbeam dance
Against my sandy shallows.

I murmur under moon and stars
In brambly wildernesses;
I linger by my shingly bars;
I loiter round my cresses;

And out again I curve and flow
To join the brimming river,
For men may come and men may go,
But I go on for ever.

This is another example of a poem that is most easily learned if you first visualize the scenes described and remember the *abab* rhyme scheme of each verse.

A *hern* is a heron; a *thorp* is a village; to *gloom* is to become dark; *cress* is a plant.

The Lady of Shalott

Alfred, Lord Tennyson

> Tennyson took the basic story for this poem from a 14th-century Italian romance about the 'Damsel of Scalot' who died for love of Sir Lancelot. It is a long poem, but it can be satisfying to learn, taking the poem scene by scene.

Part I

On either side the river lie
Long fields of barley and of rye,
That clothe the wold and meet the sky;
And thro' the field the road runs by
  To many-towered Camelot;
And up and down the people go,
Gazing where the lilies blow
Round an island there below,
  The island of Shalott.

Willows whiten, aspens quiver,
Little breezes dusk and shiver
Thro' the wave that runs for ever
By the island in the river
  Flowing down to Camelot.
Four grey walls, and four grey towers,
Overlook a space of flowers,

And the silent isle imbowers
  The Lady of Shalott.

By the margin, willow veiled
Slide the heavy barges trailed
By slow horses; and unhailed
The shallop flitteth silken-sailed
  Skimming down to Camelot:
But who hath seen her wave her hand?
Or at the casement seen her stand?
Or is she known in all the land,
  The Lady of Shalott?

Only reapers, reaping early
In among the bearded barley,
Hear a song that echoes cheerly
From the river winding clearly,
  Down to towered Camelot:
And by the moon the reaper weary,
Piling sheaves in uplands airy,
Listening, whispers ' 'Tis the fairy
  Lady of Shalott.'

Part II

There she weaves by night and day
A magic web with colours gay.
She has heard a whisper say,
A curse is on her if she stay
  To look down to Camelot.
She knows not what the curse may be,

And so she weaveth steadily,
And little other care hath she,
   The Lady of Shalott.

And moving through a mirror clear
That hangs before her all the year,
Shadows of the world appear.
There she sees the highway near
   Winding down to Camelot:
There the river eddy whirls,
And there the surly village-churls,
And the red cloaks of market girls,
   Pass onward from Shalott.

Sometimes a troop of damsels glad,
An abbot on an ambling pad,
Sometimes a curly shepherd-lad,
Or long-haired page in crimson clad,
   Goes by to towered Camelot;
And sometimes thro' the mirror blue
The knights come riding two and two:
She hath no loyal knight and true,
   The Lady of Shalott.

But in her web she still delights
To weave the mirror's magic sights,
For often through the silent nights
A funeral, with plumes and lights,
   And music, went to Camelot:
Or when the moon was overhead,

Came two young lovers lately wed;
'I am half sick of shadows,' said
   The Lady of Shalott.

Part III

   A bow-shot from her bower-eaves,
He rode between the barley-sheaves,
The sun came dazzling through the leaves,
And flamed upon the brazen greaves
   Of bold Sir Lancelot.
A red-cross knight for ever kneel'd
To a lady in his shield,
That sparkled on the yellow field,
   Beside remote Shalott.

The gemmy bridle glittered free,
Like to some branch of stars we see
Hung in the golden Galaxy.
The bridle bells rang merrily
   As he rode down to Camelot:
And from his blazoned baldric slung
A mighty silver bugle hung,
And as he rode his armour rung,
   Beside remote Shalott.

All in the blue unclouded weather
Thick-jewelled shone the saddle-leather,
The helmet and the helmet-feather
Burned like one burning flame together,
   As he rode down to Camelot.

As often through the purple night,
Below the starry clusters bright,
Some bearded meteor, trailing light,
  Moves over still Shalott.

His broad clear brow in sunlight glowed;
On burnished hooves his war-horse trode;
From underneath his helmet flowed
His coal-black curls as on he rode,
  As he rode down to Camelot.
From the bank and from the river
He flashed into the crystal mirror,
'Tirra lirra,' by the river
  Sang Sir Lancelot.

She left the web, she left the loom,
She made three paces thro' the room,
She saw the water-lily bloom,
She saw the helmet and the plume,
  She looked down to Camelot.
Out flew the web and floated wide;
The mirror cracked from side to side;
'The curse is come upon me,' cried
  The Lady of Shalott.

Part IV

In the stormy east-wind straining,
The pale yellow woods were waning,
The broad stream in his banks complaining,
Heavily the low sky raining

Over towered Camelot;
Down she came and found a boat
Beneath a willow left afloat,
And round about the prow she wrote
  The Lady of Shalott.

And down the river's dim expanse
Like some bold seer in a trance,
Seeing all his own mischance –
With a glassy countenance
  Did she look to Camelot.
And at the closing of the day
She loosed the chain, and down she lay;
The broad stream bore her far away,
  The Lady of Shalott.

Lying, robed in snowy white
That loosely flew to left and right –
The leaves upon her falling light –
Through the noises of the night
  She floated down to Camelot:
And as the boat-head wound along
The willowy hills and fields among,
They heard her singing her last song.
  The Lady of Shalott.

Heard a carol, mournful, holy,
Chanted loudly, chanted lowly,
Till her blood was frozen slowly,
And her eyes were darkened wholly,

Turned to towered Camelot.
For ere she reached upon the tide
The first house by the water-side,
Singing in her song she died,
  The Lady of Shalott.

Under tower and balcony,
By garden-wall and gallery,
A gleaming shape she floated by,
Dead-pale between the houses high,
  Silent into Camelot.
Out upon the wharfs they came,
Knight and burgher, lord and dame,
And round the prow they read her name,
  The Lady of Shalott.

Who is this? and what is here?
And in the lighted palace near
Died the sound of royal cheer;
And they crossed themselves for fear,
  All the knights at Camelot:
But Lancelot mused a little space;
He said, 'She has a lovely face;
God in his mercy lend her grace,
  The Lady of Shalott.'

A *wold* is an area of open hilly country. A *shallop* is
a type of boat.

The Charge of the Light Brigade

Alfred, Lord Tennyson

This is perhaps the best-known poem by Tennyson. It describes the charge of the British light cavalry against Russian artillery at the Battle of Balaclava in 1854 during the Crimean War. You can listen online to a very old recording of Tennyson himself reciting this poem.

Half a league, half a league,
  Half a league onward,
All in the valley of Death,
  Rode the six hundred.
'Forward, the Light Brigade!
Charge for the guns!' he said:
Into the valley of Death
  Rode the six hundred.

'Forward, the Light Brigade!'
Was there a man dismay'd?
Not tho' the soldier knew
  Some one had blunder'd:
Theirs not to make reply,

Theirs not to reason why,
Theirs but to do and die:
Into the valley of Death
  Rode the six hundred.

Cannon to right of them,
Cannon to left of them,
Cannon in front of them
  Volley'd and thunder'd;
Storm'd at with shot and shell,
Boldly they rode and well,
Into the jaws of Death,
Into the mouth of Hell
  Rode the six hundred.

Flash'd all their sabres bare,
Flash'd as they turn'd in air
Sabring the gunners there,
Charging an army while
  All the world wonder'd:
Plunged in the battery-smoke
Right thro' the line they broke;
Cossack and Russian

Reel'd from the sabre-stroke
　Shatter'd and sunder'd.
Then they rode back, but not
　Not the six hundred.

Cannon to right of them,
Cannon to left of them,
Cannon behind them
　Volley'd and thunder'd;
Storm'd at with shot and shell,
While horse and hero fell,
They that had fought so well
Came thro' the jaws of Death,
Back from the mouth of Hell,
All that was left of them,
　Left of six hundred.

When can their glory fade?
O the wild charge they made!
　All the world wonder'd.
Honour the charge they made!
Honour the Light Brigade,
　Noble six hundred!

The Last of the Light Brigade

Rudyard Kipling

Rudyard Kipling used the theme of the Six Hundred in *The Last of the Light Brigade*, which he wrote in criticism of Britain's poor treatment of its ex-soldiers. It describes a supposed visit to Tennyson by the last remaining survivors of the famous charge at Balaclava. Less well-known than Tennyson's poem, it makes an interesting contrast to it.

There were thirty million English who talked of
     England's might,
There were twenty broken troopers who lacked a
     bed for the night.
They had neither food nor money, they had
     neither service nor trade;
They were only shiftless soldiers, the last of the
     Light Brigade.

They felt that life was fleeting; they knew not that
     art was long,
That though they were dying of famine, they lived
     in deathless song.
They asked for a little money to keep the wolf
     from the door;

And the thirty million English sent twenty pounds
and four!

They laid their heads together that were scarred
and lined and grey;
Keen were the Russian sabres, but want was
keener than they;
And an old Troop-Sergeant muttered, 'Let us go to
the man who writes
The things on Balaclava the kiddies at school
recites.'

They went without bands or colours, a regiment
ten-file strong,
To look for the Master-singer who had crowned
them all in his song;
And, waiting his servant's order, by the garden
gate they stayed,
A desolate little cluster, the last of the Light
Brigade.

They strove to stand to attention, to straighten the
toil-bowed back;
They drilled on an empty stomach, the loose-knit
files fell slack;
With stooping of weary shoulders, in garments
tattered and frayed,
They shambled into his presence, the last of the
Light Brigade.

The old Troop-Sergeant was spokesman, and
  'Beggin' your pardon,' he said,
'You wrote o' the Light Brigade, sir. Here's all that
  isn't dead.
An' it's all come true what you wrote, sir,
  regardin' the mouth of hell;
For we're all of us nigh to the workhouse, an' we
  thought we'd call an' tell.

'No, thank you, we don't want food, sir; but
  couldn't you take an' write
A sort of "to be continued" and "see next page" o'
  the fight?
We think that someone has blundered, an'
  couldn't you tell 'em how?
You wrote we were heroes once, sir. Please, write
  we are starving now.'

The poor little army departed, limping and lean
  and forlorn.
And the heart of the Master-singer grew hot with
  'the scorn of scorn'.
And he wrote for them wonderful verses that
  swept the land like flame,
Till the fatted souls of the English were scourged
  with the thing called Shame.

O thirty million English that babble of England's
    might,
Behold there are twenty heroes who lack their
    food to-night;
Our children's children are lisping to 'honour the
    charge they made – '
And we leave to the streets and the workhouse
    the charge of the Light Brigade!

The Glory

Edward Thomas (1878–1917)

Edward Thomas was born in London of Welsh
parents. An established writer whose first book was
published in 1896, he did not start writing poetry
until 1914. By the time of his death at the Battle of
Arras, he had written more than 140 poems.

The glory of the beauty of the morning, –
The cuckoo crying over the untouched dew;
The blackbird that has found it, and the dove
That tempts me on to something sweeter than love;
White clouds ranged even and fair as new-mown hay;
The heat, the stir, the sublime vacancy
Of sky and meadow and forest and my own heart: –

The glory invites me, yet it leaves me scorning
All I can ever do, all I can be,
Beside the lovely of motion, shape, and hue,
The happiness I fancy fit to dwell
In beauty's presence. Shall I now this day
Begin to seek as far as heaven, as hell,
Wisdom or strength to match this beauty, start
And tread the pale dust pitted with small dark drops,
In hope to find whatever it is I seek,
Hearkening to short-lived happy-seeming things
That we know naught of, in the hazel copse?
Or must I be content with discontent
As larks and swallows are perhaps with wings?
And shall I ask at the day's end once more
What beauty is, and what I can have meant
By happiness? And shall I let all go,
Glad, weary, or both? Or shall I perhaps know
That I was happy oft and oft before,
Awhile forgetting how I am fast pent,
How dreary-swift, with naught to travel to,
Is Time? I cannot bite the day to the core.

Old Age

Edmund Waller (1606–1687)

The seas are quiet when the winds give o'er;
So calm are we when passions are no more.
For then we know how vain it was to boast
Of fleeting things, so certain to be lost.
Clouds of affection from our younger eyes
Conceal that emptiness which age descries.

The soul's dark cottage, battered and decayed,
Lets in new light through chinks that Time has
    made:
Stronger by weakness, wiser men become
As they draw near to their eternal home.
Leaving the old, both worlds at once they view
That stand upon the threshold of the new.

Legacies

Ethelwyn Wetherald (1857–1940)

 Ethelwyn Wetherald was a Canadian Quaker who lived most of her life in Ontario.

Unto my friends I give my thoughts,
Unto my God my soul,
Unto my foe I leave my love –
These are of life the whole.

Nay, there is something – a trifle – left;
Who shall receive this dower?
See, Earth Mother, a handful of dust –
Turn it into a flower.

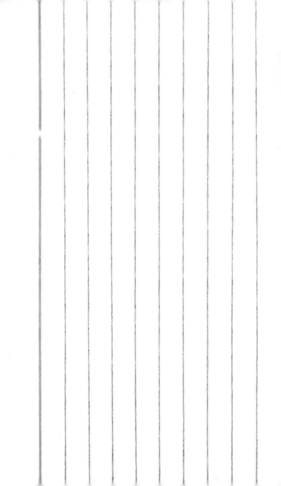

O Captain! my Captain!

Walt Whitman (1819–1892)

Walt Whitman was an American author and poet. His major work is *Leaves of Grass.* Whitman wrote *O Captain! My Captain!* in honour of the assassinated US president, Abraham Lincoln. It differs from his usual 'free verse' style seen in the next poem.

O Captain! my Captain! our fearful trip is done,
The ship has weather'd every rack, the prize we
    sought is won,
The port is near, the bells I hear, the people all
    exulting,
While follow eyes the steady keel, the vessel grim
    and daring:
        But O heart! heart! heart!
        O the bleeding drops of red,
        Where on the deck my Captain lies,
        Fallen cold and dead.

O Captain! my Captain! rise up and hear the
    bells;

Rise up – for you the flag is flung – for you the
      bugle trills,
For you bouquets and ribbon'd wreaths – for you
      the shores a-crowding,
For you they call, the swaying mass, their eager
      faces turning;
      Here Captain! dear father!
      This arm beneath your head!
      It is some dream that on the deck,
      You've fallen cold and dead.

My Captain does not answer, his lips are pale and
      still,
My father does not feel my arm, he has no pulse
      nor will;
The ship is anchor'd safe and sound, its voyage
      closed and done,
From fearful trip the victor ship comes in with
      object won;
      Exult, O shores, and ring, O bells!
      But I, with mournful tread,
      Walk the deck my Captain lies,
      Fallen cold and dead.

The 'ship' is the United States, the 'fearful trip' is
the recent Civil War, and the 'prize sought' is the
ending of slavery.

Once I Pass'd Through a Populous City

Walt Whitman

> This 'free verse' style of poetry is typical of Whitman's writings. Free verse is perhaps more difficult to memorize than poetry in the form of stanzas with a regular rhythm and rhyming lines, but this is a fairly short poem and therefore should not pose too many problems. And it is a beautiful love poem.

Once I pass'd through a populous city imprinting my
    brain for future use with its shows, architecture,
    customs, traditions,
Yet now of all that city I remember only a woman I
    casually met there who detain'd me for love of me,
Day by day and night by night we were together – all else
    has long been forgotten by me,
I remember I say only that woman who passionately
    clung to me,
Again we wander, we love, we separate again,
Again she holds me by the hand, I must not go,
I see her close beside me with silent lips sad and
    tremulous.

Homo Sapiens

John Wilmot (1647–1680)

> John Wilmot, the Earl of Rochester, was an English
> courtier, poet and satirist. Well known for his
> debauchery as a young man, after a religious
> conversion shortly before his death he gave orders
> that all his 'profane and lewd writings' be burned.

Were I (who to my cost already am
One of those strange, prodigious creatures, man)
A spirit free to choose, for my own share,
What case of flesh and blood I pleased to wear,
I'd be a dog, a monkey, or a bear,
Or anything but that vain animal
Who is so proud of being rational.
　The senses are too gross, and he'll contrive
A sixth, to contradict the other five,
And before certain instinct, will prefer
Reason, which fifty times for one does err;
Reason, an *ignis fatuus* in the mind,

Which, leaving light of nature, sense, behind,
Pathless and dangerous wandering ways it takes
Through error's fenny bogs and thorny brakes;
Whilst the misguided follower climbs with pain
Mountains of whimseys, heaped in his own brain;
Stumbling from thought to thought, falls headlong down
Into doubt's boundless sea, where, like to drown,
Books bear him up awhile, and make him try
To swim with bladders of philosophy;
In hopes still to o'ertake the escaping light,
The vapour dances in his dazzling sight
Till, spent, it leaves him to eternal night.
Then old age and experience, hand in hand,
Lead him to death, and make him understand,
After a search so painful and so long,
That all his life he has been in the wrong.
Huddled in dirt the reasoning engine lies,
Who was so proud, so witty, and so wise.

The Manly Heart

George Wither (1588–1667)

George Wither was an English poet and satirist. His satirical and polemical works three times landed him in prison, where he wrote some of his best poetry. Becoming a committed Puritan, he wrote hymns as well as poetry.

Shall I, wasting in despair,
Die because a woman's fair?
Or make pale my cheeks with care
'Cause another's rosy are?
Be she fairer than the day,
Or the flow'ry meads in May –
  If she be not so to me,
  What care I how fair she be?

Shall my silly heart be pined
'Cause I see a woman kind;
Or a well-disposèd nature
Joinèd with a lovely feature?
Be she meeker, kinder, than
Turtle dove or pelican,
  If she be not so to me,
  What care I how kind she be?

Shall a woman's virtues move
Me to perish for her love?
Or her well-deserving known
Make me quite forget mine own?
Be she with that goodness blest
Which may gain her name of Best
  If she be not such to me,
  What care I how good she be?

'Cause her fortune seems too high
Shall I play the fool and die?
She that bears a noble mind,
If not outward helps she find,
Thinks what with them he would do
That without them dares her woo;
  And unless that mind I see,
  What care I how great she be?

Great, or good, or kind, or fair,
I will ne'er the more despair;
If she love me, this believe,
I will die ere she shall grieve;
If she slight me when I woo,
I can scorn and let her go;
  For if she be not for me,
  What care I for whom she be?

Good and Clever

Elizabeth Wordsworth (1840–1932)

> The English writer, poet and academic Elizabeth Wordsworth was the great-niece of William Wordsworth. She was the first principal of Lady Margaret Hall, the first women's college in Oxford University, and founded the University's St Hugh's College.

If all the good people were clever,
  And all clever people were good,
The world would be nicer than ever
  We thought that it possibly could.

But somehow 'tis seldom or never
  The two hit it off as they should,
The good are so harsh to the clever,
  The clever, so rude to the good!

So friends, let it be our endeavour
  To make each by each understood;
For few can be good, like the clever,
  Or clever, so well as the good.

The Daffodils

William Wordsworth (1770–1850)

William Wordsworth and Samuel Taylor Coleridge (see page 60) are the founders of the Romantic Movement in English poetry, whose 'manifesto' may be found in the *Lyrical Ballads* written by these two great poets and published in 1798. Romanticism is noted for its love of the beauties of nature and the open expression of emotion, both of which can be seen in 'The Daffodils'. Wordsworth became Poet Laureate in 1843.

Wordsworth wrote this poem while he was living in the Lake District in the north-west of England. While out walking one day, he and his sister Dorothy came across an expanse of daffodils growing along the shore of Ullswater. The poet has, however, written the poem as if he was alone.

I wandered lonely as a cloud
  That floats on high o'er vales and hills,
When all at once I saw a crowd,
  A host, of golden daffodils,
Beside the lake, beneath the trees,
Fluttering and dancing in the breeze.

Continuous as the stars that shine
  And twinkle on the milky way,
They stretched in never-ending line
  Along the margin of a bay:
Ten thousand saw I at a glance
Tossing their heads in sprightly dance.

The waves beside them danced, but they
  Out-did the sparkling waves in glee:
A poet could not but be gay,
  In such a jocund company:
I gazed – and gazed – but little thought
What wealth the show to me had brought:

For oft, when on my couch I lie
  In vacant or in pensive mood,
They flash upon that inward eye
  Which is the bliss of solitude;
And then my heart with pleasure fills,
And dances with the daffodils.

When learning this poem, visualize the two
episodes the poet describes: firstly, the poet out
walking and finding the daffodils along the shore
under the trees; and then the poet in solitude in
his room.

The World Is Too Much with Us

William Wordsworth

The world is too much with us; late and soon,
Getting and spending, we lay waste our powers:
Little we see in nature that is ours;
We have given our hearts away, a sordid boon!
This Sea that bares her bosom to the moon;
The Winds that will be howling at all hours
And are up-gathered now like sleeping flowers;
For this, for everything, we are out of tune;
It moves us not – Great God! I'd rather be
A Pagan suckled in a creed outworn;
So might I, standing on this pleasant lea,
Have glimpses that would make me less forlorn;
Have sight of Proteus rising from the sea;
Or hear old Triton blow his wreathed horn.

Note that 'wreathed' in the last line must be
pronounced as two syllables 'wreath-ed' to keep
the rhythm of the line.
   Proteus and Triton are Ancient Greek sea-gods.
Triton blowing his horn causes the roaring of
the sea.

Upon Westminster Bridge

William Wordsworth

Earth has not anything to show more fair:
Dull would he be of soul who could pass by
A sight so touching in its majesty:
This City now doth like a garment wear
The beauty of the morning; silent, bare,
Ships, towers, domes, theatres, and temples lie
Open unto the fields, and to the sky;
All bright and glittering in the smokeless air.
Never did sun more beautifully steep
In his first splendour, valley, rock, or hill;
Never saw I, never felt, a calm so deep!
The river glideth at his own sweet will:
Dear God! the very houses seem asleep;
And all that mighty heart is lying still!

Westminster Bridge spans the River Thames in London.

Lines Written in Early Spring

William Wordsworth

I heard a thousand blended notes,
While in a grove I sate reclined,
In that sweet mood when pleasant thoughts
Bring sad thoughts to the mind.

To her fair works did Nature link
The human soul that through me ran;
And much it griev'd my heart to think
What man has made of man.

Through primrose tufts, in that sweet bower,
The periwinkle trail'd its wreathes;
And 'tis my faith that every flower
Enjoys the air it breathes.

The birds around me hopp'd and play'd:
Their thoughts I cannot measure,
But the least motion which they made,
It seem'd a thrill of pleasure.

The budding twigs spread out their fan
To catch the breezy air;
And I must think, do all I can,

That there was pleasure there.

If I these thoughts may not prevent,
If such be of my creed the plan,
Have I not reason to lament
What man has made of man?

'Sate', an old form of *sat*, is pronounced 'sat'.

The Lake Isle of Innisfree

W B Yeats (1865–1939)

William Butler Yeats was born in Dublin, but lived in England during his youth. Homesickness took him back to Ireland in 1891. The isle of Innisfree stands in Lough Gill in the north-west of Ireland. Yeats was awarded the Nobel Prize for literature in 1923.

I will arise and go now, and go to Innisfree,
And a small cabin build there, of clay and wattles made:
Nine bean-rows will I have there, a hive for the honey-bee,
And live alone in the bee-loud glade.

And I shall have some peace there, for peace comes
  dropping slow,
Dropping from the veils of the morning to where the
  cricket sings;
There midnight's all a glimmer, and noon a purple glow,
And evening full of the linnet's wings.

I will arise and go now, for always night and day
I hear lake water lapping with low sounds by the shore;
While I stand on the roadway, or on the pavements grey,
I hear it in the deep heart's core.

The Poet Wishes for the Cloths of Heaven

W B Yeats

Had I the heavens' embroidered cloths,
Enwrought with golden and silver light,
The blue and the dim and the dark cloths
Of night and light and the half-light,
I would spread the cloths under your feet:
But I, being poor, have only my dreams;
I have spread my dreams under your feet;
Tread softly because you tread on my dreams.

The Song of Wandering Aengus

W B Yeats

The 'Aengus' here is possibly Aengus Og, a hero of Old Irish mythology and god of love, youth and beauty. Aengus met a beautiful woman who disappeared and he long wandered in search of her.

I went out to the hazel wood,
Because a fire was in my head,
And cut and peeled a hazel wand,
And hooked a berry to a thread;
And when white moths were on the wing,
And moth-like stars were flickering out,
I dropped the berry in a stream
And caught a little silver trout.

When I had laid it on the floor
I went to blow the fire aflame,
But something rustled on the floor,
And some one called me by my name:
It had become a glimmering girl
With apple blossom in her hair
Who called me by my name and ran
And faded through the brightening air.

Though I am old with wandering
Through hollow lands and hilly lands,
I will find out where she has gone,
And kiss her lips and take her hands;
And walk among long dappled grass,
And pluck till time and times are done,
The silver apples of the moon,
The golden apples of the sun.

When You Are Old

W B Yeats

When you are old and grey and full of sleep,
And nodding by the fire, take down this book,
And slowly read, and dream of the soft look
Your eyes had once, and of their shadows deep;
How many loved your moments of glad grace,
And loved your beauty with love false or true,
But one man loved the pilgrim soul in you,
And loved the sorrows of your changing face;
And bending down beside the glowing bars,
Murmur, a little sadly, how Love fled
And paced upon the mountains overhead
And hid his face among a crowd of stars.

Index of first lines

Index of topics

Adventure

Animals

Purchased! Aug. 2/14
Chapters

Tales

Time

War

Wisdom

Work